ACTING 2.0

DOING WORK THAT GETS WORK
IN A HIGH-TECH WORLD

ACTING 2.0

DOING WORK THAT GETS WORK
IN A HIGH-TECH WORLD

ANTHONY ABESON

A SMITH AND KRAUS BOOK 2016

ISBN 978-1-57525-902-4
Library of Congress Control Number: 2015952869

Typesetting and layout: Elizabeth E. Monteleone
Cover photo: Peter Kraus
Cover design: Borderlands Press

A Smith and Kraus book
177 Lyme Road, Hanover, NH 03755
editorial 603.643.6431 To Order 1.877.668.8680
www.smithandkraus.com

Printed in the United States of America

ACTORS ON ANTHONY ABESON

JENNIFER ANISTON

Mr. Dear Abeson,

I am so proud to be a part of your WORD getting out to the young and the old who want to pursue this crazy profession. If there is any teacher on this planet to crack open the human heart to access that part . . . it is you!!!

Anthony Abeson was the first man to inform me I was funny. This news was bittersweet considering the information came just as I exited, having performed Chekhov. I came off stage and I said, "They're laughing at me." And he said, "I know. They were . . . ." Awkward silence. "Jennifer, let me tell you something: you're funny." Offended I replied, "I'm not funny, I'm a serious actress." And he said, "No, no, this is not a bad thing. Go with it. We love funny. Just understand that you can't use that as a crutch when you need to go deep." So all these years later, I guess you could say, Anthony Abeson sent me on my path, because his words, to this day, resonate in me and in my work. My instinct was to find the funny. He steered me by understanding what was inside of me before I could, and how comedy can be deepened by a dramatic moment and drama can be enhanced by a comedic approach. They're intermingled; that's life. Anthony helps his actors find the honesty in every moment. So for any actor to just have a moment with Anthony or a class with him, or by luck, have his words to read and reread, one will be twice or three times the actor for it.

I love you always and thank you always. All my love and support,

Jennifer xx

Ian Somerhalder

(The Vampire Diaries)

There are very few people in one's life who make a profound difference whether it be from tutelage or just friendly advice. Mr. Abeson gave me both. Learning and applying what is learned are two vastly different things. It takes the right teacher to offer a way in which to easily bridge the two while staying emotionally connected to whatever you find yourself doing in a professional situation on screen or stage. The way in which Anthony Abeson teaches is like no other—you are his equal, although he's going to know more than you at this point so close your mouth and listen. ... He's the only man I've met who can drop a Stanislavski quote in reference to a TV pilot and make it sound so utterly simple, making absolute sense while simultaneously making it usable to a scattered, young and struggling actor. I think about him and use his methods consistently in my work and have a life-long appreciation for his unique teaching style, Buddha-like patience and understanding. Those looking for guidance in order to make sense of this crazy business should listen to this man.

By making actors better at what they do from his studio to the stage and on the screen, Anthony Abeson's contribution to the world of theater and film should be appreciated and respected by all who reap the benefits of emotionally connected and moving performances by his former and future students.

Dilshad Vadsaria

(Greek, Revenge)

Anthony was my first acting teacher. His passion and respect for the craft always shone through in class. Anthony taught me to always have respect for the work and challenged me to find the life and humanity behind the words. He challenged me to always make specific choices. I can't express enough how fortunate I was to find a teacher and mentor who taught me what it is to raise my work, especially in a world where what we try to achieve as story-tellers is mostly overshadowed by frivolity.

RENO WILSON

(MIKE AND MOLLY)

Anthony Abeson's effect on my life and career has been profound. If you study with Mr. Abeson, you are not only becoming a versatile actor—you become a student of the history of the craft. And as an actor you constantly challenge yourself to stay in the moment, think real thoughts, and be private in public. "Your talent is in your choices." If you choose Mr. Abeson, you choose freedom and success. He is the last bastion of hope for the American actor. I am forever his disciple.

JAMES WOLK

(THE CRAZY ONES, FRONT OF THE CLASS, YOU AGAIN, LONE STAR, POLITICAL ANIMALS, ZOO)

I was fortunate enough to be told about Anthony Abeson and smart enough to seek out his class the year after college, and his work forever changed my life. His words hold a boundless amount of wisdom and the language in which he speaks is so understandable and relatable that an actor can't help but flourish and deepen their work just by talking with Anthony, sitting in his class, and now, by reading his book.

The other benefit (in addition to sharpening my tools and learning my craft as an actor) I accrued from studying with Anthony was uncovering my deeper purpose for pursuing the craft and learning to be proud to call myself an actor. His love and reverence of acting is so contagious that you can feel it down in your soul. If you are looking for deeper meaning in your work then look no further. I became truly alive as an actor after studying with Anthony and I am forever grateful to him for this.

KERRY BUTLER

(XANADU, CATCH ME IF YOU CAN, THE BEST MAN)

I wish I found Anthony earlier in my career. He is very helpful when developing a new character. He sees things that aren't on the page. The technique of fleshing out what the character is thinking is extremely beneficial. The work he does with you makes you pay attention to the details. This has helped me in many aspects of my career, on stage and in film.

ADAM CHANLER-BERAT

(THE DELIVERY MAN, NEXT TO NORMAL, RENT, PETER AND THE STARCATCHER)

In an art form so personal and so often mystifying, Anthony's approach cuts through the fog with clarity, sensitivity, richness, and options. His exercises are meant to empower the actor with confidence in the boundlessness of one's own imagination. If we're lucky, a modicum of his curiosity, generosity, playfulness, and passion will rub off on readers like me.

RACHEL BOSTON

([500] DAYS OF SUMMER, GHOSTS OF GIRLFRIENDS PAST, THE WITCHES OF EAST END)

Anthony Abeson is a true deep-sea diver into the human soul. I met Anthony when I first moved to New York City from a mountain in Tennessee at 17. I was in this giant city with a southern accent and a subway map and was led to a class that dramatically shaped my life. From the very first day, Anthony inspired me to trust my heart and instincts. In a world that encourages and rewards the external and material, Anthony remains true to the internal and intangible. With compassion, humor, and humanity, he sets up an environment where you are safe to break down walls and find your truth. He teaches it and lives it, and his teachings and life lessons are with me on every set and every step of the way.

ESAI MORALES

(BLINK, LA BAMBA, NYPD BLUE, LAW AND ORDER, CAPRICA, FAIRLY LEGAL, MAGIC CITY)

Anthony Abeson is an actor's alchemist. A sorcerer of sentiment. A medicine man of motivation. To this day his words of wisdom, quoted from sages past, reverberate in my mind and heart. Anthony Abeson's teaching technique, cultivated from his own studies with five of the great masters, not only preserves but also enhances the dynamic artistry of our craft. With Anthony Abeson, it's not just about being good at what you do, but connecting with greatness. He shepherds you to reach deep down and find things that might surprise and startle you. For me? Anthony Abeson is an endless well of inspiration. I have not gone to many acting coaches. Frankly I find some of them develop unhealthy co-dependencies with many of their students. Anthony teaches and guides in a style that allows you to think and learn for yourself. He teaches us so that we do not have to go back to him . . . but boy, do we always want to.

EMMA BELL

(DALLAS, FROZEN, FINAL DESTINATION 5, THE WALKING DEAD, LIFE INSIDE OUT)

Anthony made me want to act again. After going through many acting programs that beat one particular method into me, I began to feel restrictions around my art.

I started resenting the process of getting into character. When I joined Anthony, though, he made it very clear that "whatever way works for you, works for you." He gave me the tools from all different methods and allowed me to pick which ones worked the best for me. He is the greatest teacher and mentor anyone could ask for.

Sherri Saum

(The Fosters, Rescue Me, In Treatment, Gossip Girl)

Anthony Abeson is my secret weapon. Working with him has raised my game in ways innumerable. I don't walk onto a set or into an audition room without his principles guiding me, and I am a stronger actor for being his student.

Brendan Dooling

(The Carrie Diaries)

In 2010 this wise instructor came to me in the form of an infinitely knowledgeable silver fox named Anthony Abeson. . . . Anthony provides a nurturing atmosphere where actors can forge on through their work fearlessly because they know the "classroom" is void of judgment. He engages fully and invests himself wholeheartedly in the work of his pupils. . . . I'm blessed to have Anthony's guidance. It has certainly been a determining factor in the fruition of my recent success.

Amy Ferguson

(Hart of Dixie, The Master, Garden State)

Working with Anthony has been a pleasure from the start. He has an abundance of knowledge, a strict work ethic, and a sense of humor. . . . Somehow he manages to give every actor an individual experience, and it is always a positive one, even when we aren't at our best. "Do work that gets work." Anthony is one of the greatest teachers and persons I have ever had the honor of knowing and I would recommend him to anyone.

VICKY JEUDY

(ORANGE IS THE NEW BLACK)

Anthony Abeson's acting class has become the foundation of discipline combined with a pleasurable level of challenge and education. Anthony teaches us to exercise compassion, diligence, professionalism and respect... Through Anthony I have learned to defeat my greatest enemy: Hollywood's obsession over appearances and the desensitizing of our talent by modern technology. Thank you, Anthony Abeson, for turning my weaknesses into strengths and always believing I had the universe inside of me.

CHALEY ROSE

(NASHVILLE)

Anthony has a "no recipes" approach to acting and over the course of 2 years I watched him pull from his eclectic and wide reserve of knowledge to create coaching that is catered to each student based on their needs and ability... Anthony is a protector of the art of acting and encourages his actors to act with integrity...he's also a champion of the vulnerable actor on stage...He feels with us and for us and is proud of us when we succeed...People grow in Anthony's class...because...in his gifted hands we are safe...I am a richer, more complex, more honest human being and therefore a better actor with more places within myself to visit. I'm so excited that he's written this book.

DEDICATION

I dedicate this book to my teachers, Jerzy Grotowski, Peter Brook, Lee Strasberg, Stella Adler, and Harold Clurman, all of whom, in wildly different ways, inspired and developed my work;

To my students, past and present, who have brought me such joy and who have never ceased to challenge me to rise to the occasion of their talent;

To those actors whom I've yet to meet, who read this book: May it inspire you to cherish the precious spark within you, and to ignite others with your work;

To my editor, Amy K. Hughes, who fortified the banks of my river;

To my literary agent, publicist and dear friend, Mike Schwager, who has stuck with me literally through thick and thin, and without whose enduring faith this book would not have seen the light of day: THANK YOU!

And finally to my wonderful wife, Sherry, and my two amazing daughters, Casey and Shay. Thank you for your love, patience, humor, and support, without which I could never have completed this work. I am so blessed and proud to have you as my family.

TABLE OF CONTENTS

INTRODUCTION: THE PROBLEM

Something precious is being destroyed from our lives.
—Anonymous lament from the dawn of the
Industrial Revolution as an entire lifestyle was
being swept away by the relentless intrusion of machinery.

The American actor's talent, like that of any artist, derives to a great extent from sensitivity: sensitivity to the power of suggestion, to the partner, to the senses, and so on. Today, in the early years of the technological revolution, this sensitivity is under assault by a variety of factors, not the least of which is technology itself. At its worst, it enables people to experience each other and the world through screens that filter out the human, replacing it with wizardry that numbs the imagination to all but the most extreme depictions (explosions, sex, violence, special effects), trapping viewers between the sterile and the puerile. It's inevitable, therefore, that as we spend more time with our faces buried in our devices, we're also losing our sensitivity to the rich nuances of human communion. Phone use is up for operating apps, watching videos, listening to music, playing games, and taking photos, but down for human conversation. This unprecedented replacement of the human with the technological seems to be gradually shifting who we are, threatening to turn us quasi-bionic. Closely paralleling what's happening to our natural environment, it constitutes a cultural climate change, threatening our human nature just as climate change endangers planetary nature. The resulting anomie erodes our ability to empathize with real people, and what it means to be human slips further from our grasp toward extinction. As Tennessee Williams foresaw many decades ago: "The moths are dying. . . . / Enemies of the delicate [are] everywhere" ("Lament for the Moths").

Since this alienation afflicts the general population, it also naturally affects actors, who, because they're immersed in the same culture, may succumb to the same distractions, lack of empathy, and loss of humanity as their fellows. But actors can inflict greater damage because of their power to affect their audience. Let's not forget that actors inadvertently tempted people to smoke by making it seem glamorous. In a similar way, the loss of the actor's humanity can lead directly to a loss of the audience's. Conversely, the more human the actor, the more humane the audience. Because incidents of inhumanity seem to be on the rise (witness the steady increase in reports of deliberate cruelty to animals and people), we need our actors to be, if anything, even more human than ever, to form a bulwark against the brutes.

How I Hope This Book Can Be Part Of The Solution

Whether you are just embarking on your journey as an actor or whether you've been on that path for many years, your talent and your audience confer great responsibility upon you—something you can lose sight of under the many pressures we face as actors in America. Use this book as a reminder of your calling. Use it to either supplement your classes or, if necessary, alert you to the dangers in them. Dip into it for ideas when you're stuck or for inspiration when you're down, for the challenges are many, and you will meet them even in the very material with which you are confronted. I hope that this book can help you to program your internal GPS toward the North Star of your artistry, so you can raise the material, any material, not lower yourself. I hope to encourage you to reveal the truths of your characters, not just display yourself, and to do, not just talk. In short, I want to empower you with practical tools with which to do good work that gets work "in the room"—work on the stage and screen that inspires all of us, that arouses not prurience or violence but that precious "something," intangible but of inestimable value, that is "being destroyed from our lives": our humanity.

PART I
IN THE MIRROR

ACTORS: Before you go into "the room," don't
forget to remember yourselves.

The Sorcerer, from the Cave of the Trois-Frères,
illustrated by Henri Breuil.

CHAPTER 1

"MAGICAL PREHISTORIC TRIBE DISCOVERED

LIVING IN 21ST CENTURY!"

If you saw that headline, wouldn't you want to meet one of them? Well, look in the mirror. If you're driven, salmon-like, against the current and the odds to perform, then you're one of them: a carrier of precious, ancient, magical performance DNA.

When the human race lived in caves, the hunt was crucial for survival. To ensure success, an act of sympathetic magic was performed the night before, in which the stalking and slaying of the animal was acted out. Most of the clan was content to sit and watch, but a few unusual ones (even then we must have seemed odd to our fellows) were impelled to perform. One put on the skin of an animal, another picked up a spear, and together they performed "The Hunt." I believe such an early actor is depicted in the ancient cave painting pictured above, whose very setting in the Cave of the Trois-Frères in southwestern France is imbued with a sense of the magical. As the mythologist Joseph Campbell wrote in *Primitive Mythology*, it was, for some twenty thousand years, "one of the most important centers of magic and religion—if not, indeed, the greatest—in the world." Herbert Kühn, a German historian, described the experience of entering the cave, sixty feet below the earth's surface, at the end of a tunnel some forty yards long and no broader nor higher than one's shoulders: "We wriggle forward on our stomachs, like snakes. The passage, in places, is hardly a foot high, so that you have to lay your face right on the earth. . . . You cannot lift your head; you cannot breathe. . . . Then, suddenly, we are through. . . . The hall in which we are now standing is gigantic. . . . From top to bottom a whole wall is covered with engravings . . . of the beasts that lived at that time."

"And above them all, predominant . . . some fifteen feet above the level of the floor," Joseph Campbell writes, is the "'Sorcerer of Trois Frères'. . . . a god of sorcerers . . . one who has donned the costume of a god; . . . as we know, and see amply illustrated in the lore of modern [indigenous peoples], when the sacred regalia has been assumed, the individual . . . is a conduit of divine power . . . he is a manifestation of the god . . . embodied in some of the shamans themselves."

INVOCATION: THE SORCERER'S LEGACY

The following, which I wrote in honor of the cave painting and of the ancient potencies of acting it represents, is to remind you of who you are: remnants of an ancient race of sorcerer-magicians, inheritors by genetic transmission from your ancestors of a tendency to perform and to become other people. It becomes next to impossible to intimidate actors who are in touch with the size that their ancient heritage confers upon them.

> Actors: behold your great Original,
> The Sorcerer of Trois-Frères Cave.
> Engraved upon the ancient rock,
> First known portrait of our kind,
> Caught illumined in an act of magic and per-
> formance
> By the flash-bulb suddenness of the artist's
> glance—
> He blinks at us from out across the Reindeer
> Age
> And treads the ancient dance, suspended,
> With 20,000 Stone Age years
> Startling in his eyes.
>
> At our collective dawn,
> In great conventicles of darkling potency,

Strobed by flames and thundered by the drum,
Humanity was kept alive
By actor-shaman-priests like him:
They burned, igniting audience,
But like the ancient bush were not consumed:
Artaud's actors at the stake, signaling through
the flames,
Transporting their audience to that place
From whence we come, toward which we all
repair
In grace and ecstasy and death.
They acted out the hunt gone well, so that it
would,
Ensuring the survival of our race.
They danced and sang the Sun from Solstice
death,
And planted hope, an evergreen, in people's
hearts,
That their Sun and they'd survive.

Actors: we are the Sorcerer's apprentices,
carriers of that ancient strain of potency and
magic.
It is our birthright, it lies within our cells,
And drives us to perform/transform.
This remnant of our ancient calling, like a star-
fish limb,
Retains the vital spark of our Progenitor,
And could become the fullness of its source.

May we, as starfish actors once again, growing
in a starfish way,
Assume our place as crucial to the people's
lives—
Ensuring their humanity's survival,
No longer through the Stone Age hunt for
flesh,
But as runways for the human spirit,

Effecting magic once again, the alchemy whereby
Our audience is made more human, more humane,
As we become the sons and daughters of the Human Race:
New Sorcerers for an Age of Stone.

PART II
IN PERSPECTIVE

A tip of the hat to some of the seminal figures
who have contributed to our art.

CHAPTER 2

IN PRAISE OF STANISLAVSKI

Before Konstantin S. Stanislavski (1863–1938)—Russian actor, teacher, and founding artistic director of the Moscow Art Theatre—there were actors but no acting. His contribution was so profound as to be akin to the discovery of fire. In its earliest days, the human race recognized the importance of fire as a source of light, warmth, and protection from predators. But once a fire had burned out, our prehistoric ancestors had no idea how to recreate it, so they had to rely on chance: the odd strike of lightning, a forest fire, whatever. So it was with good acting. Before Stanislavski, people could recognize and value it, but they had no idea how to re-create it, so most actor training consisted of literally repeating the externals of good performances. "When so-and-so played this part, he raised his arm on this line and spoke in this tone." The parallel is exact: a desire to re-create what was recognized as "good," and a lack of understanding of the process that gave rise to it. No wonder Stanislavski quit drama school after three weeks. He was frustrated by the disconnect between the beautiful acting results he'd been promised and the lack of an effective process to achieve them.

Stanislavski set out on a voyage of discovery, observing many good actors in numerous countries, trying to figure out what, despite linguistic and cultural differences, they had in common. (His first observation: that every good actor, even in moments of heightened emotional connection, was relaxed. Conversely, sweating and straining were hallmarks of the bad ones.) Stanislavski was the first person to try to understand something that, until then, had been ephemeral and often ascribed to "inspiration" (essentially, a lightning strike). No one had ever sought to rigorously observe the miraculous phenomenon of good acting, much less to systematically investigate the circumstances that could nurture it, the ingredients essential for the creation of it, and the processes that could lead to it.

Stanislavski literally created the craft and then advanced it in numerous ways, experimenting, exploring, and changing his mind throughout his career, refusing to be dogmatic. His mantra was "No recipes—whatever works" (see Chapter 12). He arrived at certain principles of the actor's process that continue to work and guide generations of actors today, many of which inform the contents of this book, which, "like virtually all others in the contemporary . . . theatrical 'canon' is derivative [of] or sparked by that great Russian master" (as Harold Clurman wrote in his introduction to *Advice to the Players*, by Robert Lewis). No longer did we have to be like hunter-gatherers waiting for an electrical storm to ignite good work. No longer would we be condemned to trying to summon inner magic by means of outer symptoms. No one, since the dawn of time, had harnessed the alchemy of inspiration. As far as our work is concerned, Stanislavski was the first "technician of the sacred."*

* This phrase comes from Jerome Rothenberg's 1968 anthology of indigenous writings, *Technicians of the Sacred: A Range of Poetries from Africa, America, Asia, Europe and Oceania.*

CHAPTER 3

AN EXCHANGE BETWEEN GROTOWSKI AND STRASBERG, ACROSS THREE DIFFERENT DECADES

GROTOWSKI

In 1968 I sat transfixed, along with my fellow participants, on the second floor of the Centre Dramatique National du Sud-Est in Aix-en-Provence, France, listening to Jerzy Grotowski's take on the nature of the actor's impulse, as part of a "stage," or workshop. This being Grotowski, the visionary Polish theater director, it was sometime in the middle of the night—our sessions began at four every afternoon and lasted till well past midnight. Much of the work was practical, interspersed with the theoretical, as it was this particular night. And yet, for some reason we felt, more than usual, something magical and mysterious was being disclosed to us, and the atmosphere reflected that.

Grotowski likened the actor's impulse to that of the lion, which waits in a state of total relaxation until a gazelle comes within range. At that instant the lion changes suddenly, from relaxation to attack, shifting its hundreds of pounds of muscle and bone from one extreme state to another. This phenomenon Grotowski attributed to the role of the "partner" (in this case the gazelle). (For a more thorough discussion of the concept of the partner, please refer to Chapter 24, "Working with a Partner.") As opposed to circus lions, which leap mechanically, this lion could be said to have been leapt by the gazelle: Its action was triggered impulse as opposed to rote repetition.

The implications for the actor seemed profound. Rather than repeat an action mechanically (an acting product), which would quickly lose the illusion of the first time (and devolve into what Lee Strasberg called "general emotion"), I could react to whatever the partner could say and/or do that would trigger the action (a reacting process). My previous training, Method, involved repeating the sensory elements of an affective memory. Here, the focus was off me and on the partner, which felt liberating and immediate. It also seemed, as Grotowski was fond of saying, "pure," insofar as there wasn't a division in the process between thinking of doing and then doing. (The original meaning of "holiness" was "wholeness.") How can the audience receive you totally if you're divided? But when you're "gazelle-leapt" there's no such division: The instant the prey is within range, the lion is in the air.

Grotowski felt that the theater was the only place where such purity could be attained. In the social realm the mercurial flow of pure life is disrupted. We bump into someone we're bummed to see, our first reaction ("yuck"), while pure, is not socially acceptable, so we instantly cover it with one that is ("Hi, how are you?"). Similarly, introductory phrases like "Let me be honest with you" or "Let me tell you a joke" grind life to a halt while everyone starts adjusting to what's coming next. This conditioning takes a toll on the actor's ability to respond to stimuli instantaneously, purely, without a gap between impulse and response. Grotowski's work at that time was concerned with the elimination of that gap, which T. S. Eliot referred to as "the shadow" in his poem "The Hollow Men":

> Between the idea and the reality,
> Between the motion and the act,
> Falls the shadow.
>
> Between the conception and the creation,
> Between the emotion and the response,
> Falls the shadow.

But where in all this was the role of the sensory, which Richard Boleslavsky (see Chapter 7) had called "the bait for the emotions"?

STRASBERG

Fast-forward about a dozen years. As a member of the Directors Unit of the Actors Studio, I was listening to Lee Strasberg discuss impulses. After the session I approached him to discuss what seemed to be similarities between his take on impulse and Grotowski's. At his invitation, we continued later on at his home in one of those Dakota-like, pre–World War II buildings, an architectural gem. Strasberg had a genuine, deep love of learning, which was evident right at the entrance to his apartment. You had to walk down a narrow hall, made narrower still by the seemingly endless rows of bookshelves, bursting with volumes,   running along the entire length of the corridor, which opened out into a spacious living room, also surrounded by bookshelves, overlooking Central Park.

It was a beautiful fall, late afternoon, and the trees were spectacular in their autumn colors. Lee punctuated our conversation about impulse by playing old recordings of the same classical composition by various pianists, illustrating the differences in their interpretations and drawing a parallel to actors' interpretations of classical roles. I've always thought that Strasberg was never fully acknowledged for his comparative analysis of the actor's work vis-à-vis other artists and disciplines. For me he shed much light on the importance of the relationship between the *what* (the material) and the *how* (the interpretation.)

Returning to impulse, I asked him for his take on Grotowski's theory of the lion being "leapt" by the gazelle. He said that essentially he agreed with it but with one critical condition. "And what's that?" I asked. And he replied, "The lion has to be hungry." *Bam*. There it was: the relation of the sensory to impulse. How fitting that Lee, having made the sensory the cornerstone of his work, would supply it.

We spoke of the great Russian actor-director Yevgeny Vakhtangov, whose production of *Princess Turandot* combined exuberant theatricality with emotional truth. Stanislavski stopped the final dress to rush to Vakhtangov's deathbed to congratulate him and bestow upon him the title "my greatest pupil." Vakhtangov, age thirty-nine, died three days later. As the twilight deepened, our voices became tinged with regret that such talent was cut short at such an early age. The brief silence, as that of "an angel passing," descended on us, while outside Lee's windows the trees were glorious, their fall colors glowing in the sunset, dying brilliantly—like Vakhtangov.

PART III
IN THE CULTURE

The following section is meant to help you negotiate the challenges of trying to practice your
art in this historical moment.

CHAPTER 4

A GUY WALKS INTO A BAR . . . AND TALKS ABOUT ACTING

I'm always amazed at the disparity between people's awareness of athletic skill versus acting technique. Go anywhere in
America, particularly around the time of big sporting events like
the Super Bowl, the World Series, or the Olympics, and you'll be
treated to an informed, highly technical analysis, often supported
by statistics, of the abilities, offensive and defensive strategies,
and prospects of various teams, coaches, and players. The development of athletic talent is also followed attentively, whether
it be the impact of a change in batting stance, golf swing, or left
hook, a return from injury, or a new starting lineup.

This very high level of public awareness is matched by an
equally high level of skill among the athletes themselves. Even the
players on the lowest-ranked professional teams have achieved
a basic level of excellence that far exceeds what any amateur
could. This is no accident. Nor can it be separated from the fact
that when players or coaches fail, they're booed and often fired
or traded—and the possibility of such consequences has a tendency to concentrate the mind. It is said that Shakespeare learned
what worked and what didn't by having his mistakes booed by
the groundlings.

WHERE ARE THE GROUNDLINGS WHEN WE NEED THEM?

Just as there's a connection between an informed public and
athletic excellence, so too is there one between an uninformed
public and mediocrity in the acting profession. The person who

was just holding forth on the reasons for a particular team's defeat in the Super Bowl will clam up when asked to analyze the level of work on the latest hit TV series.

This refusal of the public to evaluate acting with the same fervor applied to sports has the expected effect on actors, directors, and producers. Rather than concentrating the mind, the anything-goes attitude lets it off the hook, freeing those responsible for a show to act with impunity, allowing the focus to be more on commerce than on art, without fear of public outrage.

It's time to get the pitchforks. In the Middle Ages, when bread was considered the "staff of life," if a baker was found to have adulterated it with poor ingredients, there were riots and the offender was punished. My hope is to provoke outrage of a nonviolent but no less compelling sort by exposing the damage done to the public by an entertainment diet that leaves them overfed on style and undernourished on substance. Why not? The exposure of the use of steroids and other performance-enhancing drugs among professional athletes provokes national outrage, prompting congressional hearings and heated discussion of the damage inflicted on the young by these supposed role models, now tainted by their use of illegal substances.

Your Higher Calling

The ability of actors to impact our youth is even greater, for while athletes can wow us in the moment, actors—"athletes of the heart"—can reflect and reveal the human condition, humanizing, teaching, moving, and inspiring us for the rest of our lives.

But many actors abdicate their higher calling by watering down their work, substituting "hotness" for humanity and talking for living, while getting a free pass from the paying public. Yet the harm this degradation of acting does to an audience, especially the young, is far greater than that of all the steroids ingested by all athletes combined, because that kind of acting, in high-def and Dolby, goes directly into the bloodstream to the heart and consciousness of the people, clogging their arteries, blocking their hearts, and numbing their spirits.

Raising the level of acting awareness in the general population, one audience member at a time, will enable spectators to evaluate acting as perceptively as they do sports. But how? Let's encourage the audience to see beneath the exteriors of the actors and ask themselves certain questions: *"Do I believe her/him?"* *"Do they know what they're talking about?"* *"Are their eyes dead or is the material alive in them?"* No training other than being human is required to answer these questions (we all know when we're being lied to), and the understanding they would yield would lead to change. No longer would we have to accept substandard work due to a lack of informed criteria. Bad acting, no matter how attractively packaged, would be revealed for the rip-off that it is. A more discriminating audience will demand better acting, raising the level of nourishment we ingest. We truly are what we eat.

CHAPTER 5

ANNE FRANK WASN'T HOT

When Ezra Pound said "Artists are the antennae of the race," he was referring to the way that turbulence in the arts—the rise of dissonance in music or distortion in painting—has often preceded and presaged major upheavals in society such as wars, revolutions, and economic distress. But today that dynamic has been reversed. Instead of artists reflecting what's about to befall the people, it is now the people who reflect what has already befallen the artists.

HOT OR NOT

As an acting coach, I'm writing specifically about actors, who are being cast more and more for their looks and less and less for their talent. The continual display of perfect bodies on television and movie screens has contributed not only to an epidemic of eating disorders but also to spiritual disorders. Increasingly, young people evaluate all humanity as either "hot" or "not."

Some years ago I spoke with a twelve-year-old girl about Anne Frank's *Diary of a Young Girl*, which she was reading for school. I asked how she liked it so far, and she replied, "She was a liar." "How can you say that?" I asked. "Because she said that a lot of boys liked her—no way." "Why not?" "She wasn't hot."

I'm convinced that this kind of thinking represents one of many canaries fluttering their last breaths in our cultural coal mine, warning us of the toxic atmosphere we're inhaling from the criteria and values of the entertainment industry. Where once casting seemed to strive for a combination of looks and talent, the equation now appears to have shifted radically toward the former at the expense of the latter, particularly with regard to film and television aimed at the youth market. A while ago I coached a young woman on a screen test for a television project. Afterward the casting director told me that she had been, "hands down, the best actress of the bunch. But we went another way." "Why?" I asked. "Because the girl we went with is a Victoria's Secret model," he said, as if that were the most obvious explanation imaginable.

Consider this breakdown (character description) for a film audition: "Must be strong actress . . . and look great in lingerie." Or this: "Just beneath her ivory snow exterior is a babe-a-licious ready to unleash her inner hottie." Nor is this limited to young women. It turns out that what a network really wanted to see wasn't the two monologues that a young actor named James and I had prepared, but rather what he looked like with his shirt off, holding an automatic weapon. This degraded perception of the actor has steadily permeated the acting culture, from the casting director whose response to a talented young man upon his arrival in L.A. was "Whiten your teeth and bulk up in the gym" to the actors who, getting the message loud and clear, particularly from those who hold the keys to employment, are tempted to exercise their bodies more than their talent.

This takes a terrible toll on young performers who are being led to perceive their "hotness" as the route to success. "Wow," said an actor to one of my students at a screen test for a soap opera. "You do real acting. When I go back to L.A., I'll be doing the 'pretty-face, six-pack-abs' acting." This sort of self-image condemns them to being treated as throwaways rather than renewable resources. Consider the ever-faster cycle with which the industry feeds its insatiable hunger for pretty young people, gobbling them up and spitting them out. This cycle is self-perpetuating: The more entertainment options, the more need for "hotties," who, internalizing the industry's conflation of looks with talent, try to market their looks right into employment, often without any training at all. But the dragon eats its tail: Undeveloped talent used is talent used up. Even if an individual achieves some initial "success," whatever personality trait or look seemed to have worked the first time will be milked unceasingly until it gives out and the industry goes looking for a replacement. The discard is then abandoned to the tender mercies of the market place, ill-equipped to repackage itself, because the actor has fused with a self-portrait that's no longer marketable.

In an interview I was asked this question: "Director Elia Kazan hired Vivien Leigh for *Streetcar* because of her beauty. So what's wrong with beauty still informing casting decisions today?" It's a valuable question. Leigh was, indeed, beautiful, but she was cast just as much, if not more so, for the luminous fragility she radiated and her ability to animate her character with those qualities—that is, her talent. And the public responded to that. No one perceived Leigh as merely "hot." Her exterior expressed her interior. As T. S. Eliot said, humans are "joined in spirit and body, / And therefore must serve as spirit and body. / Visible and invisible, two worlds meet" in us. But nowadays the industry's call to serve involves more of the flesh and less of the spirit.

This trend is not lost on the young. That twelve-year-old girl wasn't born seeing people as either "hot" or not. Her take on them was warped by the distorting lenses held up to her eyes by various aspects of popular culture; and more young eyes and values are being distorted every day. Beauty, in a grotesque distortion of the old saying, has indeed become "its own reward"—one that is warping the values, hearts, minds, and spirits of our youth.

CHAPTER 6

NUDITY

No discussion of the industry's emphasis on looks can be complete without a consideration of the question of nudity. I understand how unnerving it can be to be told at an audition, "By the way, this part requires nudity." You want the job, and you don't want to come off as "difficult" or a prude, but you also don't want to feel exploited.

First of all, let's keep in mind that not all nakedness is sexual. Think about St. Francis: It was said that sometimes when he preached, in his ecstatic yearning to get closer to God, he would tear off all his clothes in front of the congregation. Or consider Lear on the heath: "Come, unleash you lendings."

Years ago I shot a film where I played one half of a couple who become so caught up in the materialism of the corporate rat-race that they head out to the country to reconnect with nature—their own human nature and Mother Nature. While there they encounter a Native American woman, who acts as a spiritual guide to each of them in different ways, helping to lead them back to their authenticity. For my character, there came a moment in the film rather like a crossroads. I was either going to take the leap into a new life or not. Standing at the edge of a cranberry bog, the Native American woman disrobed and jumped in. It was clear that she expected me to do the same. I hesitated, struggling with all my old values and prejudices, and then I, too, stripped naked and dove in. Far from feeling exploited as an actor, I felt deeply that this was a kind of baptism for my character.

What I'm trying to do here is offer some guidelines for navigating really tricky territory. If you feel you can trust the director and if you can truthfully say that full or partial nudity is crucial to the revelation of character, relationship, situation, or plot, that it's safe, organic, and artistically justified, then by all means do it. If, however, it serves none of those purposes, then it's prurient and exploitative, and while it might advance your career, it would be at a price: That's what you would become seen as and known for; it would be expected of you and increasingly difficult to say no to. I'd turn it down if I were you, just as a student of mine did the other day. She was thrilled to have booked the lead in a horror film. Throughout the audition process no mention was made of nudity. When she arrived on set, however, she was informed that her part would now require it. She refused, and was replaced, and I agreed with her decision. Not only was nudity not justified by the script, her trust in the entire project was undermined. How many other "surprises" would be in store for her?

Another thing to remember: You have something else going for you—your talent. If your work is so good that they really want you, they're going to negotiate the nudity requirement. Countless times I've coached actors whose audition magically reduced "full nudity" to one shot of a bare back on a closed set. If, on the other hand, all you bring to the table is your physique, don't be surprised if that's all they want to see.

Leonardo Da Vinci said, "The soul chooses to dwell in the body because that's how it can feel and express itself." If all you're asked for is your body, without your character's soul, then that tells you something about where that project's coming from—and going. I'm not rejecting nudity out of hand. Just make damn sure that by displaying your flesh, you're revealing the truth.

CHAPTER 7

CONSUME. REPRODUCE. OBEY.

My students often ask me how to spend their time creatively outside acting class, and in this chapter and the next, I'll pass on to you the advice I give them. Believe me, if it were up to our culture, you would be so infected by the irresistible media images of hot young people having such fabulous fun wearing, drinking, driving, reading, watching, and using things that famous, hot people have that you'd want to buy it all so that you too could be like them. But you're not like them. Resist the undertow that would pull you into that world. Detach and see it for what it is: a world of consumerism. The graffito that I used as this chapter's title sums it up succinctly.

You're not consumers, you're artists, you can create. It's only those who can't create who must either own or destroy. Your job is to enrich your soul, not the wallets of those who would profit from addicting you to the new and the hot and the fear of being not. The richer your soul, the richer the contribution you'll make to your audience. For you, and all the actors who strive to retain their creativity in the midst of a culture that is, to quote the old hymn, "rich in things and poor in soul," I have the following suggestions.

UNPLUG

Unplug yourself from all your devices and distractions for some part of your day. Remember, distraction is one of the most common occupational hazards of our profession. It's a major source of tension (excess energy) in the actor, and the only antidote is concentration, which can channel that energy. There's a reason the seminal acting teacher Richard Boleslavsky (Stanislavski's pupil during his early period and the teacher of three of my teachers, Lee Strasberg, Stella Adler, and Harold Clurman), long before today's technology, began with "Concentration" in his book *Acting: The First Six Lessons*. Numerous studies have affirmed that the incessant consumption of information (11.8 hours a day for the average American) is wrecking people's ability to concentrate. Consider how often your best ideas have come to you in times of mental stillness. So what will happen to your creativity if all your emailing, texting, IM-ing, Tweeting, and Facebook postings drown out the silence that allows your creative voice to emerge? Consider these words of T. S. Eliot: "Where is the wisdom lost in knowledge?/ Where is the knowledge lost in information?"

NOURISH YOUR ARTIST

Replace the fleeting data from your devices with what's eternal: humanity. Feed on the beauty of the elderly couple holding hands as they help each other across the street, a mother with her baby, toddlers chasing pigeons, children playing, a young girl, all in purple, flying out of her house to wave at a passing bus. This is our raw material: humans being human. How can we follow Hamlet's advice to the Players to "hold as 'twere the mirror up to Nature" if we're too distracted by our technology to observe it? The more acute your perception of humanity, the more acutely you'll perceive the humanity of your characters. Take out your earbuds for one minute so you can hear, if only for an instant, the cry of a gull—its lament connects us to Chekhov's Nina and reminds us that Manhattan is still, despite everything, an island.

WAKE UP. STAY DANGEROUS.

When you resist the graffito's impetus to "Consume" (as for "Reproduce"—I think I'll leave that one alone), you are already refusing to "Obey." Do you remember Hans Christian Andersen's story "The Emperor's New Clothes"? How the emperor had been scammed, because his wonderful, expensive clothes didn't exist?

How he'd paraded himself naked before the whole town, to show off those clothes, supposedly visible only to those who were smart enough? No one had the guts to state the truth except a little child, who yelled, "But he doesn't have any clothes on!" You, the artists, are that child, or at least you should be. You should be sharp as tacks, perceptive as hell, and not easily duped. You should see past the surface of things and reveal what's underneath. Your calling requires it of you. If you don't unhook yourselves from the incessant craving to "consume," you'll be sucked in by the compulsion to "obey": impotent, unobservant, passive, sedated, distracted, and too high to be dangerous—just the way the culture wants you to be. Don't believe me? Check out this ad for a phone company: "Talk and surf the web at the same time!" As if people weren't distracted enough, the phone's hype offers a way for you to increase your ADHD and decrease your focus on your partner. It's profitable for the company, costly for your humanity. Don't fall for it.

Hang Out with Giants, Not Pygmies

Instead of texting, read the texts of the great playwrights and theoreticians of acting. Instead of watching YouTube, watch great films with great acting. How many of you have seen *Requiem for a Heavyweight* or *Marty*? Instead of watching reality shows, go out and watch reality; observe human beings being human. Immerse yourself in what Stanislavski called "the only true, creative genius, Nature." Instead of playing games on your devices, go to museums and see that you're not alone, that you stand in a long line of artists who have struggled with the same great task you are charged with: to capture the life of the human spirit.

And speaking of museums, read Tennessee Williams's poem "The Dangerous Painters," which says the masterpieces in museums are behind heavy gilt frames and red velvet ropes because if they were seen where they were painted, in the artists' studios, raw, immediate, and accessible, they would evoke "the goat-like cry of 'Brother'."

That's your job—to evoke that cry.

CHAPTER 8

FINDING THE RECESS IN THE RECESSION

Artists are dreamers, and what they dream about
is money.
— *Tennessee Williams*

Long ago a dear friend of mine finally booked his first Broadway musical after years of the usual hand-to-mouth performer's existence. Thrilled to finally decorate his apartment, he did so with a vengeance. The first room he completed was extravagantly elegant and lush. Then the show closed, shortly after opening. When I visited him soon afterward to offer my condolences, his apartment said it all: There, beyond the sumptuous room, were the other rooms, all barren, with only wooden orange crates for furniture.

While many working people are now experiencing a similar bust after the boom, taking part- or full-time jobs far outside their chosen profession, accepting pay cuts and reduced hours, we actors can take grim satisfaction in saying, "Been there. Done and doing that. Welcome to our world." Collectively, our long experience in hand-to-mouth existence strengthens our ability to survive economic downturns whether personal, national, or global. Here are some ideas for doing so.

DEVELOP YOUR TALENT SO SOMEONE WILL WANT TO USE IT

Instead of stressing about lost income, focus on the increased opportunity to develop your talent. Try this formula: Divide your time in half; spend half looking for work and celebrate the other half as a windfall opportunity to do what you've never had time for before. Read plays. Mount scenes, one acts, or even full-length plays with your friends in someone's apartment. While it's obvious that the best way to get better at something is to practice doing it, many actors don't act unless they have an audition or a job.

Concentrate on developing your strengths and eliminating your weaknesses. Many actors have admitted to me a fear of certain characters, such as having to be super sexy or emotionally available or tough and edgy. You know which ones scare you. During times of full employment there never seems to be enough time to develop them. Now there is. Take advantage of it.

TARGET PRACTICE

In addition to developing your talent in these ways, work on marketing it as well. Now is the time to gather all that disparate footage from indies, shorts, and student films to see which ones are suitable for a reel. Even if you currently don't have enough money to produce a reel, you'll have gotten the time-consuming gathering and sifting stage out of the way, and you'll be ready when you're flush again. Likewise, read the trades to get more savvy about the biz, update your resume, and check in with your agent. Watch plays, films, and television to see who has your job and why.

HUNGRY ENOUGH?

Finally, the down times provide an opportunity to seriously reflect on whether you want this career badly enough. Use this time to check your appetite for acting, which is one thing that cannot be taught and without which you'll never survive in the business let alone succeed in it. Unless and until you achieve lasting success, tenuous employment alternating with periods of unemployment will be your lot. If you can emerge from this time more fervent in your belief that this is what you *must* do, no matter the challenges, then you will have gained from the severity of this crucible. If, on the other hand, the prospect of long-term economic insecurity freaks you out more than acting delights you, take this opportunity to flee. You will look back on this recession and thank it for starkly revealing your priorities.

For those of you who choose to stay, remember: While your vessel is, perforce, becalmed, this is the time to scrape the barnacles from her hull, because when the winds blow again, and they will, there will be no time for maintenance. Then, along with the poet John Masefield, in his poem "Sea Fever," you will say:

> I must go down to the seas again, to the lonely
> sea and the sky,
> And all I ask is a tall ship and a star to steer
> her by,
> . . . for the call of the running tide
> Is a wild call and a clear call that may not be
> denied.

And the star you steer by is neither your money (or lack thereof) nor your day job (if you still have one). How blessed you are not to be defined by them. If you lose them, your identity is still intact. You're an actor, and your star is the recession-proof light within you, a light "the world can neither give nor take away": your talent.

CHAPTER 9

How Working with Jennifer Aniston Leads, Inevitably, to the Need for a National Theater

Serious practitioners of any craft are likely to be fascinated by the insoluble. Mathematicians have struggled to find solutions to certain problems, some dating back centuries. Likewise, many of us in the acting field have wrestled long and hard to resolve the apparent contradiction between the melancholy of Anton Chekhov's plays and his admonition that they're comedies. Even Stanislavski had difficulty with this, incurring the wrath of the writer, who complained that Stanislavski was turning the characters in *The Three Sisters* into "crybabies."

The problem of finding the humor in Chekhov has been with us for more than 100 years. Imagine my astonishment, then, when in the mid-1980s, as I was directing scenes for the final projects at the High School of Performing Arts, a teenager, seemingly without effort, found the truth and the humor in *The Three Sisters*, causing laughter in the audience. That teenager was Jennifer Aniston, and despite the magnitude of her accomplishment, she was not happy. As she recounted later (a version of this story also appears in Marlo Thomas's book *The Right Words at the Right Time*):

> Anthony Abeson was the first man to inform me that I was funny. This news was bittersweet considering the information came just as I exited, having performed Chekhov. I came off

stage and I said, "They're laughing at me." And
he said, "I know. They were. . . . " Awkward
silence. "Jennifer, let me tell you something:
you're funny." Offended, I replied, "I'm not
funny, I'm a serious actress." . . . He steered me
by understanding what was inside of me before
I could, and how comedy can be deepened by a
dramatic moment and drama can be enhanced
by a comedic approach.

This intuitive understanding and the ability to apply it to
Chekhov would have been remarkable to encounter in anyone,
but was even more so in a teenager. Such a talent deserves to
work with giants, to have a shot at being, perhaps, her genera-
tion's outstanding interpreter of Molière's heroines. But we may
never get to see that because our culture is more alive to using
talent than developing it, and because we lack what almost every
other "developed" country has—a national theater.

Scotland didn't have its own, separate Parliament until
1999, but by 2006 had already launched the National Theater of
Scotland. The United States of America has existed for nearly
250 years, and we're still without our own and missing out on
the expression of national identity it would provide. Of course,
we don't need a national theater for established stars like Jennifer Aniston to perform in plays, and many famous actors have
and will continue to take to the stage. But those opportunities
are the exception, not the rule. In England it's normal for movie
stars to alternate between stage and screen, and that normalcy
permits a workmanlike focus on the creative process and not on
the hoopla. Can you imagine the media circus and frenzy that
would accompany any play that Jennifer might seek to do? That
alone could discourage anyone from undertaking such a project.
But if we never get to see her in the plays of Chekhov, Molière,
or O'Neill, everyone loses. Jennifer loses because the development of her talent depends on the greatness of her material, and
we lose because we'll never experience the unique contribution
she could make to and through these giants. Martha Graham was
very clear about such loss: "Because there is only one of you in

all of time, this expression is unique. And if you block it, it will never exist through any other medium, and it will be lost. The world will not have it."

This is true for all the incredibly talented actors who've had their talent more used than developed. Unless and until we have a national theater where our great national resource of talent is nurtured and developed, our actors will not achieve the world-class stature of which they are capable, and our national identity will remain unexpressed, resulting in the loss of even quintessentially American parts to actors from other countries. Remember our profound shock when foreigners started taking over iconic American companies? Well, it's happening now with iconic American characters, as we'll see in Chapter 10.

PART IV
IN THE CLASSROOM

This section is meant to help you get the most out of your acting classes, while alerting you to some of the truly abusive and manipulative practices that can harm your talent and damage your soul.

No, Romeo's Not a Guy Just Like You

Q: *What do Abraham Lincoln, Teddy Roosevelt, FDR, Richard Nixon, Elvis Presley, and Martin Luther King, Jr. have in common?*
A: They have all been played by actors from the U.K., which has a rich repertory and national theater tradition.

Were there no American actors with the size or stature to play these larger-than-life American icons? What does that say about us? It may directly reflect our lack of a broad and deep infrastructure of genuine repertory companies or a national theater to offer our actors opportunities to work on such parts.

Deprived of the development and "extension of self" that regular alternation between stage and screen provides, our actors are frequently encouraged by the industry to play "close to self" or, as it is often expressed, "just be yourself." This all too often results in self-portraits. But the actor's job is not to display him-or herself, but to reveal the truth of the character. If we paint only self-portraits again and again, what are we? Can you imagine Rembrandt or Picasso painting only self-portraits? Beethoven or Mozart composing only the "Me" symphonies? Shakespeare writing only autobiographical plays? Yet this is often what film and TV scripts require and is, therefore, the key to employment.

But it's arrogant and career-crippling to bring every character down to our own street corner, as Stella Adler used to say. If we repeat our self-portrait enough times we become caricatures of ourselves, while much of our talent to become other people lies fallow and rots. Self-portraiture denies the basic human truth that we are different depending on whom we're with, be they parents, friends, teachers, children, lovers, et al. This is how we are in real life. It's not phony, it's human. In each situation it's still us, but different aspects of us are brought out in different ways by different partners and circumstances.

Self-portraiture deprives the actor of what Stanislavski described as the joy of the "complete and utter transformation into another human being; a kind of re-incarnation." Many actors continue to use characters as mirrors rather than windows, though, as Stella Adler used to proclaim, "Romeo's not a guy just like you." While you must, inevitably, start with yourselves, you shouldn't necessarily end with yourselves. Create neither a self-portrait at the expense of your character nor a pasted-on external character at the expense of your soul. Find a third, as-yet-unknown possibility: a character, written by the author, to whom you give your life.

The industry will never see us as right for many different parts until we develop the many different parts of ourselves, until we balance their perception of what we look like with who we can become. Unless we demonstrate that although we might be narrowly marketable by virtue of our type, we are infinitely usable by virtue of our talent. It was said of the Italian actress Eleonora Duse that when by a brook, uncannily, she would ripple. When her lover spied her walking over a hill with some Russian wolfhounds, for a moment he couldn't tell them apart. It wasn't about her "look," but rather about whom she could become. Nowadays it's about what we already look like.

We must recognize that to avoid having our talent used narrowly, we must develop it widely, by regularly tackling the great roles of dramatic literature (those that a national theater could provide). Absent that exercise, we'll continue to succumb to the primacy of type over talent, allowing the transformation strand of our ancient performance DNA to wither, leaving the impression that all we can paint are self-portraits.

CHAPTER 11

IDEAS

One reason for this excessive self-portraiture is our lack of exposure to the realm of ideas. The golden age of Greek drama concerned itself with the conflict between humanity's need for free will and the destiny ordained by the gods. Shakespeare was fascinated by the striving for power and the effect it had on those who achieved it. Many of the plays of the 1930s were concerned with class struggle and socioeconomic inequality, while those of the 1960s burned with antiwar, antiauthoritarian, countercultural revolutionary fervor. Stanislavski continually stressed the importance of ideas to the actor's craft, insisting that the primary and unifying responsibility for everyone involved in a production was the expression of the playwright's idea, the very thing that gives the theater the power to "change people's minds." And now? Sadly, it's a rare actor indeed who's conversant and comfortable with ideas. Today, more often than not, when I ask actors in class to identify the idea in their material, they answer with a noun—"love," for example—and I must repeatedly explain that "love" is not an idea, whereas "love conquers all" is.

A KICK-ASS JOLT OF ADRENALINE

Part of the blame can be ascribed to the quality of much of today's film and theater criticism, once a fertile ground for ideas. Read the reviews written by one of my teachers, Harold Clurman, in *The New Republic* (1948–52) and *The Nation* (1953–80) to see what I mean. Many of today's "reviews" are utterly devoid of ideas. For example, a "review" of a recent film called it "a kick-ass jolt of adrenaline!" What the hell does that tell you about the ideas expressed in the film? What clues does it offer as to what the film is actually about? If the critics don't examine a film's ideas, then a film isn't necessarily compelled to have any. We can see where this leads in the many music videos with hot-looking singers and amazing imagery, neither remotely connected to the ideas of the song. In one, while the lyrics express how hard it is to love again once your heart has been broken, the singer wanders the Grand Canyon, sometimes riding, sometimes leading her horse, blissfully oblivious to the emotional connection the lyrics could and should have for her and for us. But her hair sure looks hot.

Uncovering the Idea

If you are under forty, this is probably what you've been raised on, and you're suffering from a type of malnourishment that will stunt the growth of your characters and make them anemic replicas of yourselves. Fight this by asking, "What is the writer saying to the world?" Once you know that, you'll know what part of that idea is embedded in your character, which will immediately give it size, richness, and dimension. In Bertolt Brecht's play *The Caucasian Chalk Circle*, let's say the idea is, "Sometimes the powerless can be more humane than the powerful." (I use "let's say" because deciding on the idea is an act of interpretation; remember, you're interpretive artists, an aspect of your talent that is often unasked for.) There's a scene in which the Governor's Wife is getting ready to flee an attack by revolutionary forces. All her servants are rushing about trying to keep up with her orders about which dresses and jewelry to take. (I've condensed the scene here.)

Governor's Wife
Quick open the trunks! I'll tell you what I need. . . . The green one. And of course the one with the fur trimming. . . . Don't tear the sleeves. . . . I'll kill you, you bitch!
(She beats the young woman.)

ADJUTANT

Please make haste, Natella. Firing has broken out in the city.

GOVERNOR'S WIFE

. . . How's Michael? [Her child] Asleep? . . . Then put him down and get my little saffron-colored boots from the bedroom. I need them for the green dress.

ADJUTANT

Natella, you must leave at once!

GOVERNOR'S WIFE

Why? I've got to take this silver dress—it cost a thousand piasters . . . (*rummaging desperately*) I simply cannot find the wine-colored dress. . . . Take the dresses to the carriage. (*She's pulled out by the Adjutant.*)

SERVANT

Madam! (*Runs towards the child, picks it up and holds it a moment.*) They left it behind, the beasts. (*She hands it to Grusha.*) Hold it a moment. (*She runs off following the Governor's Wife.*)

When the other servants tell her to put him down ("I tell you, if he had the plague he couldn't be more dangerous"), Grusha replies, stubbornly, "He hasn't got the plague. He looks at me. He's human!"

LETTING THE IDEA INFORM THE CHARACTER

See how this scene encapsulates the idea we proposed above, and how each character contains an element of it? The Governor's Wife stands for all those folks whose power and money have led them to prize possessions over people (including even their own children). Grusha stands for those who have neither money nor power but do have humanity. See how the idea forces you to think outside the box of yourself, making it impossible to merely paint a self-portrait? It turns the material from a mirror ("Romeo's a guy just like me") to a window on humanity, forcing you to look further afield than yourself ("I know people like this"). If you're playing Natella without understanding the idea, you may be in danger of saying, "But I would never behave like that." Perhaps not, but she does. You're not a Governor's Wife, but you must get over this limitation in your experience and start to create her from within, via your imagination, and without, via observation.

Without adding idea-interpretation to your tool belt, you'll be clueless as to what your characters stand for, condemned to painting one more self-portrait, shrinking larger-than-life characters down to your level—which is why directors go to the U.K. to cast MLK, Jr., Elvis, Teddy Roosevelt, FDR, Nixon, and, twice now, Abraham Lincoln. A lack of ideas in your material may not be your fault, but it is your responsibility. To return ideas to the forefront of your thinking about your material and your characters will be to return size to your work and iconic parts to America.

CHAPTER 12

NO RECIPES—WHATEVER WORKS

I count myself fortunate to have been exposed first-hand to a wide variety of acting techniques, including those of Lee Strasberg, Stella Adler, Harold Clurman, Jerzy Grotowski, and Peter Brook. Having studied all those approaches, I've been, in a sense, inoculated against any one acting recipe. I follow what Stanislavski said most succinctly: "No recipes—whatever works." As Harold Clurman explained in Robert Lewis's *Advice to the Players*, "There is NO ONE RIGHT WAY. . . . The Stanislavski system is . . . not a dogma." Despite this, however, there seems to me to be an increased reliance on recipes/dogma in the acting community.

ONE-SIZE DOESN'T FIT ALL

Perhaps you're familiar with the well-known definition of insanity: repeating the same thing but expecting different results. A student of mine, a single mother, experienced this first-hand, as described in an email she sent to me.

> I took the summer intensive at the _____ Studio. It was super expensive, and after paying for my son's camp, I used the rest of my savings to pay for it because I figured I needed to get back to studying in some way, shape or form. Anyway, I had a hard time with the method. I sucked and

> I know the teacher thought I did as well. But I
> wanted to tell her I'm capable of better, it's just
> that I was trying to stay true to their method and
> it was not working for me. They said, however,
> that if you continue with the two-year program
> it will all come together.

This is exactly what Stanislavski warned us about. This program took a young mother's savings and disrespected her individuality, not only by trying to force her talent into a cookie-cutter mold but also by making her feel bad about her work. Then they dared to ask for still more of her money. *Training should adapt to the actor, not the other way around.* Any training worth its salt cannot be fetishistic or one-size-fits-all. If the actor's not improving, it's up to the teacher to change methods and arrive at a way that's effective. It is not only rigid but punitive to make the actor feel it's his or her problem the "method" isn't working. Acting instruction should be practical and immediately useful. It certainly should not take two years and a summer to bear fruit.

Here's an example of how blind allegiance to a recipe can violate basic logic: A student of mine was working on a scene in someone else's class in which she played a counselor at a camp who has to confront another counselor about his skinny-dipping with the campers. She began the scene and was stopped immediately: First she had to do a sense memory of the grass. Why? Because without experiencing the texture, smell, and look of the grass, she wouldn't believe she was in a camp. That's a perfect example of the fetishism that often permeates actor training in this country. The actress didn't need the grass to confront the counselor. All she needed was to picture him being inappropriate with the kids in the water: She'd be catapulted into the scene, with belief in the situation and driven by a need to confront him, which is, after all, what the scene is about. But that wasn't the way they worked in that class; there they always began with sense memory—which in this case gave her the grass, but neither the trigger, the connection, the intention, nor the scene.

UNLOCKING TALENT

I think of each actor who comes before me as a unique event in the universe, a treasure-chest filled with glittering jewels it is my challenge and responsibility and honor to unlock. And there is no skeleton key. Even if one key works for one actor one time, it won't always work for that same actor, much less for all actors, for all material, all the time. Those of us who teach or direct have to have a backup plan for when what we're sure will work doesn't. As Strasberg explained, while a pianist knows that a key will always sound when struck, sometimes our piano "closes its lid, rolls away and says it's not in the mood."

Instead of a simple keyhole waiting for a master key, those of us fortunate enough to work with talented actors are more likely to be confronted with a combination lock requiring several different approaches and directions. If you find a teacher with only one way of working, don't place your talent in his (or her) hands forever, for one way will never be remotely sufficient for all acting problems (including your own). And for any teacher to thrust his limitations on a wide variety of actors, again and again, only damages their talent and shames our calling.

A teacher's allegiance should be to the development of talent, not to any one particular way of working. We teachers should always seek to enlarge our menu rather than shrink the talent with which we've been entrusted. Actor training is not about the teacher, but about the artists who come to us trusting that somehow, with patience, ingenuity, and grace, we'll be able to find the ways to ignite their talent.

CHAPTER 13

YOU CAN'T PUKE IF YOU HAVEN'T EATEN:
SOME THOUGHTS ON EMOTION

Many acting teachers, I'm sorry to say, pressure actors, overtly or covertly, to achieve emotional results (see also Chapters 14 and 17). It's tough enough that the industry will often do that, but even tougher when teachers, who should be teaching you an emotional process, pressure you instead to come up with an emotional product.

The process is based on nature: It's obvious you can't have a fruit without a tree. Apply this to human nature and the actor's challenge of evoking emotional results, and the parallel is exact: The emotional "fruit" has to be grown by some kind of "tree." Stanislavski put it another way. He said grabbing for an emotion is like grabbing for a child: They'll both run away, as they're easily frightened. His solution? Take out a lollipop. For the actor, this would be what we call a "choice," the "tree" in our analogy. If, however, you succumb to the pressure to show an emotional result, and wind up skipping over the tree (the choice) to produce the fruit, several things will occur. You'll start to tense up with the effort, because while you can just react to a choice, you have to act when there's none. And with nothing in your stomach, but still under pressure to produce, your acting will resemble the dry heaves—not a pretty analogy but an accurate one. You'll be straining to produce, but nothing will come out. How could it? Nothing went in.

It is important to remember that our emotions are not under our conscious control and consequently do not respond well to pressure. Need proof? We can't stop loving people no matter how hard we try. And we can't make ourselves love people, even when we wish we could. We get angry when we try to stay calm, and we blush when we're trying to hide our embarrassment. So abandon any attempt to directly control your feelings; it's futile. Instead, let's try to lure them indirectly, using what Boleslavsky called "bait."

It's important to demystify the entire area of the actor's emotional availability. It is far easier and lighter to achieve than is commonly thought, because we are hard-wired to connect quickly and deeply to specific stimuli. How long does it take you to connect emotionally to that song that reminds you of a certain ex? How long to react to a whiff of the scent she used to wear? To her picture? Not long at all, right? A mother who lost her son in Afghanistan told a reporter that it was hard to predict when her tears would come. They could be triggered by random images or sounds, even by a smile, a song, or a joke. As she said, "There will always be something that triggers it." And that is my point: It is a process of triggering, not of producing, and a well-chosen choice will serve as that trigger.

REAL AND IMAGINARY CHOICES

The choice does not have to be real. In fact, we often have to make it up, because the nature of the material is far from our own lived experience. W., an actress in my class, was working on a monologue about how her father had hung himself. (Her real father hadn't.) The character was clearly meant to be upset, and that implicit pressure for an emotional result was making her tense. I asked her to stand on a chair. Puzzled, she did. "Cut him down," I said. "Take an imaginary knife and saw through the rope." Immediately she relaxed, because the choice transferred the energy that was tightening her into an action and an object that connected her instead. As Stanislavski said, "The small truth leads to the big truth."

When faced with seeking an emotional result, try to translate the product into a process that takes the pressure off you and puts it squarely on the choice. The menu of choices, real and/or imaginary, is huge: sights, sounds, tastes, smells, touches, music, thoughts, actions, objects, and so on. Part of your job is to know what kinds of things work for you. The director wants you "disgusted"? Choose what you know will disgust you. She wants "more"? Amp up the choice, not your instrument, and make the choice more disgusting. If the choice is disgusting, you'll be disgusted. If the choice is more disgusting, you'll be even more disgusted.

REPEATING THE CONNECTION

And then there's the problem of not just getting emotionally connected, but repeating that connection. (Let's remember that the French for "rehearsal" is *répétition*.) If there's any secret to our craft, perhaps it's what a nineteenth-century American actor, William Gillette, called the ability to repeat "with the illusion of the first time." Sometimes a choice will seem to wear out with repetition. When that happens, actors will often blame the choice and seek a new one. But I've discovered that most of the time the choice was just fine, it was the actor's process that was flawed. Under the pressure of multiple takes or eight shows a week on Broadway, actors, unconsciously, will often start trying to repeat the feeling, not the trigger. But that's "grabbing at the child," and it will run from you.

Most of the time the choice can be infinitely repeatable as long as it's delivered correctly to your system. I worked on a TV movie with an actor who had to make an emotional speech in front of a gymnasium full of people. He told me that despite more than twenty takes, he was able to connect emotionally every time, because he repeated the choice and didn't try to repeat the feeling. All W. has to repeat is cutting that rope. It'll work every time.

CHAPTER 14

THE DISPLAY OF YOUR "ISSUES"
IS NEITHER APPROPRIATE NOR ART

Let's continue our discussion of the choice with the example from the preceding chapter. But let's say that W. *did* have a father who had killed himself, and she didn't want to use the experience as her choice because it would have been just too painful. One thing that can cripple an actor is the continual use of certain real, lived choices as a source of emotional connection. Just recently my student C. had to begin a scene in the state of having experienced someone suffering. She made it clear that while she had a very strong personal past to draw from, she knew better than to do so. She made a choice up and it worked just fine. Yet the belief that the route to real feelings lies only through the real, traumatic past has become so entrenched, it permeates the general population and even popular culture.

Years ago I shot a television pilot in which I played the part of an acting teacher whose first "lesson," ironically, involved urging my students to begin by remembering the most painful experiences of their lives. The thought of large numbers of impressionable young people getting the idea that that's what acting is all about terrified me, and I bitched and moaned until they let me write my own stuff (which was neither clever nor deep, but at least it wasn't going to hurt anybody).

"AIN'T NOBODY'S BUSINESS BUT MY OWN"

This emphasis on the painful past persists in many acting schools to this day. Significant numbers of students have come to me from elsewhere, profoundly shaken by having to "rip their guts out" in class, supposedly in the pursuit of "emotional truth," "not holding back," "total honesty," and so on. Underneath such fine phrases, however, lies an unspoken value system that exalts real, past pain over the use of the imagination; it would encourage C. to "go there" anyway, despite her reservations. This was the case with S., a student of mine who was asked by a teacher if she'd ever done anything she was ashamed of. "Yes," S. replied. "Tell us about it," said the teacher. "I'd rather not," S. said. The teacher persisted—"No, you really ought to"—on and on, relentlessly, despite S.'s obvious resistance until, while still refusing, she was crying hysterically. The teacher then triumphantly displayed the tears as validation of her approach. This is wrong on so many levels. First, if an actor truly doesn't want to rip scabs off emotional wounds, it's his/her right to refuse to do so. Second, it's unnecessary anyway, because the imagination is quite capable of creating the necessary emotional connection. Furthermore, whether or not the actor chooses or refuses to use the real lived past is his or her business, and the choice doesn't need to be discussed in order for it to work. It's a perversion of the acting process to confuse it with personal disclosure. And finally, hysteria's not acting; it's hysteria, and its inducement against an actor's will is abuse.

PRIVATE IN PUBLIC

This emphasis on dredging up and prying into the actor's painful, personal experiences has resulted in the perversion of certain exercises as well. Take for example the "private moment," which Strasberg devised to strengthen the actor's ability to be, in Stanislavski's words, "private in public." Strasberg defined it thus: "I asked these actors to do something that they do in life, but which even in life is so private that . . . when anyone comes in, they have to stop doing it" (quoted from *Strasberg at the Actors Studio*, edited by Robert H. Hethmon). Sounds reasonable, right? But this exercise has often been twisted into something much more inclined toward hysteria, self-indulgence, and prurience.

After two years with me (that's our limit), a wonderful young actor went to a well-known, reputable, Method-based acting class, where he was assigned a private moment and came in with what seemed to me to be a perfect example of Strasberg's definition. An adherent of an Eastern religion, he chants as part of his private meditation; it was something he'd never done in front of others before. He brought in elements from his room to bolster his sense of privacy and chanted. Scary as it was to share something so private, he struggled at first and then succeeded. After a few minutes he was truly alone in his "room," chanting as fully and privately as ever. But his work was rejected as not being sufficiently "emotional."

PUBLIC IN PUBLIC

Another young woman's private moment, however, was accepted. And what did that young woman do? She stripped to her underwear, ate a lot of donuts, and threw up. *Really*. The original intent of the exercise was wrenched from being private in public to a humiliating, self-indulgent display of exhibitionism: public in public.

This dangerous perversion of the goals of actor training has also led to a complete skewing of the focus we bring to the exercises and the criteria by which we evaluate them. The actress revealed that she suffered from bulimia, and the students and teacher responded with questions about that: "How long have you had this?" "When did you first notice it?" "Is it painful?" The point of the exercise—"Did you succeed in achieving a sense of privacy?"—was lost.

This tendency towards the lurid and the confessional has always been an unfortunate component of actor training. But it has been exacerbated by the "reality" and talk shows that disgorge daily amounts of humiliating self-display into the culture, bombarding our sensibilities and tempting us to equate narcissistic self-indulgence with art, when it is, in fact, merely narcissistic self-indulgence. It's up to us, as artists, to resist this downward spiral. If your training involves forcing you into areas you know in your gut are harmful, leave. That poor young woman's public display of her bulimia, while titillating, had nothing to do with developing her privacy or her talent, and everything to do with taking advantage of her "issues" for shock value. Far from being creative, it was, in fact, exploitative.

CHAPTER 15

GETTING CONNECTED TO THE MATERIAL

At this point, it's instructive to remember Stanislavski's evolution regarding the use of the real, lived past, which he termed "affective memory" (literally, memory that affects us). In his early period he called it the "cornerstone" of his technique. Many years later, however, after exhaustive research and experimentation, he famously changed his mind and called it, instead, the "last resort," largely because of the hysteria and tension the constant recycling of painful memories produced in the actors. "Last resort" doesn't mean "never," but it should satisfy two conditions: It doesn't hurt you, and it is a legitimate parallel that doesn't trivialize the stakes and the circumstances. As long as that's the case, go ahead and use a memory from your real past. I did.

THE USE OF THE REAL

My father died in 1983. Soon thereafter I had to do a monologue from John Osborne's *Look Back in Anger*, which begins, "Anyone who's never watched somebody die is suffering from a pretty bad case of virginity." I *had* watched my father die, and I used the memory of it because it was a legitimate parallel. I remembered the look in his eyes as the end approached, and how the coldness of death gradually crept over him till it reached the tip of his nose. I wasn't substituting the death of my turtle for the death of my father, and it didn't hurt too much. In fact, it felt rather nice to remember my last moments with Dad again.

I had another reminder of how sometimes the use of the real simply works, period, when I was coaching a young man for an audition, which included the following passage: "She's given up her life for me, OK? She's not only been my mother—she's been my father, my teacher, my coach. She worked two jobs when I was a kid to put food on the table. And she still managed to . . . buy me new cleats when I needed them."

When I started to work on this speech with him, he calmly announced, "I don't need to do anything with that speech." "Why not?" I asked. "Because that's my mom. That's who she was, that's what she did." Neither he nor I needed to resort to technique to connect with the situation—we had the connection. He wasn't "sick" so he didn't need "medicine." (Many actors tend to distrust anything that comes easily to them and feel compelled to apply a checklist of techniques anyway. But remember: "If it ain't broke, don't fix it.")

PROBLEMS WITH THE USE OF THE REAL AND POSSIBLE SOLUTIONS

A young woman had to enter a scene upset that her boyfriend had just dumped her. She started out imagining that it was her real boyfriend, but in this case the choice of the real wasn't working. As she put it, "I'm kinda over him now, and it wouldn't really bother me if he dumped me. In fact, I'm thinking of dumping him." The boyfriend was the wrong choice, but she kept trying to force it to work because it was "real." Nonetheless, the boyfriend was clearly a loaded issue for her, so I decided to tweak the real choice by throwing out the bathwater but keeping the baby.

This entailed separating the choice from its baggage. "Forget the current situation with your boyfriend," I told her. "What about when you first met and it was wonderful? How'd you meet?" There was a pause. Her whole demeanor changed, and she said, "In an elevator." Pause. "It seemed like anything was possible back then." By this time she was tender and dreamy. "That's who just dumped you," I said, and it was enough to catapult her into the scene.

USE YOUR SENSITIVITY TO THE POWER OF SUGGESTION TO MAKE BELIEVE

Another problem with the use of the real is that sometimes, no matter how we tweak our choice, life can change it from useful to useless, and your work should not be held hostage to circumstance. A few weeks after we'd separated the baggage from the choice, the young woman told me that although the revised version had worked for a while, things had gotten so much worse with the boyfriend that now it was impossible to even think of him, much less use him. But that hadn't stopped her from trying though. Again and again she'd tried to force herself to connect to the loss of him, because he was real, without success. (Remember that earlier definition of insanity? Continuing to try what's already failed and expecting a different outcome?) You're not a piece of wood, nor is your choice a nail that'll go deeper into you the harder you hammer it. Your instrument's not dumb; it will resist going to an unpleasant place, and the more you try to force it, the more tension you'll create within yourself and the more of an obstacle you'll create between you and your connection to the situation. This clearly was a job for that oft-neglected alternative to the real choice: the imaginary one.

"Forget the boyfriend," I told her. "Let's just imagine 'Mr. Right'. Accept this imaginary reality as real: that you've met the man you want to spend the rest of your life with, the man you want to marry, have children, and grow old with. Finally, after all this time, you've met 'the one'. Don't even try to visualize him; like a developing photograph, he'll appear, bit by bit. For now, just react as if you've met your soul mate." And because she's an actress, and therefore susceptible to the power of suggestion, she began to react truthfully to the imaginary partner. She became romantic, glowing with her newfound love. "Now imagine that he dumped you." With that, she connected to the heartbreak of her character and began the scene already experiencing and believing in her imaginary circumstances. And she was able to endlessly repeat that connection because it was immune to the fluctuations of her relationship with her real boyfriend.

THE COMBO PLATTER: PASSING THE REAL THROUGH YOUR IMAGINATION

Sometimes there's a real person who's the right choice to use for your partner but whose circumstances are wrong for the scene. An actor was required to connect to the death of his father, but his father—unlike mine—was alive and kicking, and the actor had never lost anyone close to him. So we passed his real dad through his imagination and pictured him in a hospital bed, hooked up to all sorts of machines, with tubes in his nose, arms, mouth, and half his body weight lost, along with his hair. That young actor became immediately connected to the imaginary reality of his father at death's door. I had them share a few tender last words, and when his father passed, he totally owned that imaginary circumstance. He didn't have to keep dredging up and recycling some genuinely painful, irrelevant experience from the past, nor did he have to start from scratch and create an imaginary father—he already had one whom he loved. Without tension, without doing damage to himself, and rather quickly at that, he created a past that his character owned, that he didn't, by means of his talent. He did not have to resort to trying to warp something of lesser significance into standing for the death of his dad, as in the following examples.

SQUARE-PEG-IN-A-ROUND-HOLE SUBSTITUTIONS
(NO, THE DEATH OF YOUR TURTLE ISN'T EQUIVALENT TO THE DEATH OF YOUR PARENT)

Years ago I was sitting on a city bus with a distinguished American actor, a venerable member of the Actors Studio, discussing affective memory. I asked him how he could possibly apply it to the line "I saw Indians smash my dear parents' heads on the pillow next to mine," from Arthur Miller's play The Crucible.

What, I asked him, could he possibly use from his real, lived past to enable him to "own" those lines? Wouldn't he have to make it up? "No," he said. "You could use the time your mother slapped you, and it might have felt just as bad."

Whoa. Crazy, right? A choice is never going to work if it reduces something so large to something so small and irrelevant. Here's another example: An actor had to commiserate with his friend who had lost his job on Christmas Eve and had to tell his children there would be no presents for them. His work was so strange, however, that I had to stop him and ask what kind of a choice was he using. "I'm remembering the time I broke a rib," he told me, as if that made utter sense.

You can't make this stuff up. And that's the problem, he should have. Do you see the madness of these approaches? How they trivialize the material and drain the power of the characters' experiences out of an allegiance to the real, lived past? How they can tempt actors to lose faith in and neglect their imaginations by implying that only the real can work for them? There's simply no way that our real-life experiences are capable of satisfying the demands of all, or even most, scripts, and yet we try to force them to. This demeans not only the writing but also your talent by implying that you can't create, you can only recycle. And because it stunts your imagination, it becomes a self-fulfilling prophecy. But it's our imaginations that have allowed us to make believe since we were kids. Remember, acting's the ability to live truthfully in large imaginary circumstances, not the ability to replace the imaginary with the small reality of our own lives.

So, in order to "own" these two imaginary realities, the smashing of your parents' heads by Indians or the loss of your friend's job on Christmas Eve, without jamming square pegs of nonparallel personal experiences into the round holes of the characters, we have to apply an old technique to which I've given a new name: F.I.O. (Flesh It Out). In the next chapter we'll discuss this and apply it to these two examples.

CHAPTER 16

F.I.O.: FLESH IT OUT

I have a scar on the fourth finger of my left hand. It's there now, in the present, but it comes from long ago when I played Richard III and was cut while rehearsing a sword fight. We all have scars, and each one has a story behind it, proof of the anomaly that the present contains the past. This is as true of our material as it is of our bodies. When you think about it, so much of what our characters say, though spoken in the present, springs from their past—a past actors rarely think about, though they used to. I remember hearing years ago about how the great English actress Sarah Siddons (1755–1831) prepared for Lady Macbeth by acting out references to the past in her and others' lines so that, in her words, they would have "associations" for her.

THE WORDS ARE JUST THE TIP OF THE ICEBERG OF THE PAST

Stanislavski also stressed the importance of the actors' keeping their characters' pasts alive. For example, here he describes how an actor in the title role might flesh out the following lines from Molière's farce *Tartuffe*: "Last week, his conscience was severely pricked / Because, while praying, he had caught a flea / And killed it, so he felt, too wrathfully."

> Can you really see this picture of Tartuffe's goodness and tenderheartedness? How he jumped out of bed in the middle of the night, stark naked, shivering with cold, lit a candle and told his servant . . . of the disaster that had occurred,

> how they both looked for the flea for a long time,
> how Tartuffe, having found it, warmed it with
> his breath, trying to revive it, how he then put it
> on a clean sheet of paper and spent the night in
> prayer and bitter tears. That's the kind of picture
> . . . you should see with your inner eye when
> you try to make Cleante feel reverence for this
> saintly man.
>
> —*Stanislavski in Rehearsal*, Vasili Toporkov

This step of fleshing out the past stems from our need to truly believe that we know what we're talking about. If we do, our eyes will be alive; if we don't, they'll be dead. What's more, we're not talking about some weird acting technique, but about how people really talk. Watch a friend describe something that's happened to him in the past—you'll see the truthfulness in his eyes. Finally, there's the ethical component: If you don't know what you're talking about but you say it anyway, you're lying, and our job as actors is to tell the truth to the people.

So I have devised the acronym "F.I.O." to identify this process: flesh it out. If the text is the skeleton, then F.I.O. involves putting flesh on its bones. But first you have to stop the muscles of your tongue and notice when you're talking about things you've never experienced, but your character has. That's a critical step. So many actors don't even pause to notice the past in their lines in their frenetic desire to keep talking. We clutch the words when there's nothing else going on in our performance to hold onto.

Fleshing Out the Past by Picturing

Once you've slowed down enough to smell the roses of the past, there are several ways to flesh it out. If your imagination is fertile, then most of the time all you have to do is think about what you're saying, and images will arise in your mind's eye (see Chapter 19, "How Ordering Takeout Can Help Your Career"); we'll see that the material is alive in you, and we'll believe because you will. In one of my classes we worked on some sides with the following lines.

HENRY
I'll tell them about stealing the street sign,
and stealing Mr. Powell's car . . .

LUCINDA
Not how we streaked by the police station. Or
what we used to do back in your house when we were
alone . . .

We have two choices. We can just say those lines, painting the words with typical actorly line readings, or we can picture the past they come from, which would infuse those words, and therefore the characters and the atmosphere, with the nostalgic warmth, truth, and colorful life the scene requires. Try it: Picture in your mind's eye each of these events, watch them like movies, and then notice how that generates belief and imagery that pours into and enlivens the lines—giving you belief that you know what you're talking about. That's part of your gift as actors, to be susceptible to the power of suggestion.

But feed yourselves well; don't make the images boring or a compilation of data. There's a vast difference between saying to yourself, "It was 43 degrees the night of November 17, 1995, when we ran naked by the police station at the corner of Lafayette and Colby," and picturing yourself and your naked partner, shaking your freezing body parts outside of the police station, yelling "You have the right . . . to be impressed" and then fleeing when the cops begin pouring out, only to slip on the ice and fall, laughing hysterically, rolling in a naked heap, while struggling to get back up on your feet. Can you feel the difference? The data doesn't percolate the images into belief nearly as well. This is an example, in actor terms, of the truth of the saying "Knowledge not lived is sin."

HOW WE F.I.O.'D THE CRUCIBLE SCENE

We applied this technique in class to *The Crucible* line I quoted in the preceding chapter: "I saw Indians smash my dear parents' heads on the pillow next to mine." We began not with any of the students' substitutions from their real lives (unlike the actor remembering his mother's slap), but with an acceptance that we were in seventeenth-century New England. We pictured the bedroom we shared with our sleeping parents and imagined we were awakened by a sense that something wasn't right. Looking out the window from bed we saw, silhouetted in the moonlight, the figures of several Indians going by outside. Before we could warn our parents, we heard the door open, and we pretended to be fast asleep. Peeking out through half-open eyes, we saw the Indians steal into the room and raise their tomahawks, the blades glinting in the moonlight. Our mother's scream awakened our father, who tried to fight but was scalped instantly, the blade making a horrible sound as it connected with his flesh. His bloody scalp was thrust into our mother's face, and then it was her turn. Suddenly we were confronted with an Indian's face right in front of ours. He raised his tomahawk, we silently prayed, and then, just as suddenly, he was gone.

When we returned to the line, everyone was connected to it, because they believed they knew what they were talking about. And because they believed, they were believable. The entire exercise took less than five minutes. What's more, those images will stick to those words forever. This is much lighter and more effortless than trying to wrestle the square peg of a slap into the round hole of a scalping.

FLESHING OUT THE PAST WITH ACTIONS

But sometimes the disconnection between our imaginations and our instruments prevents us from really feeling that we've experienced what we say we have. At those times we've found it useful to flesh out a written reference to the past through actions, an approach often applied to a similar problem in the teaching of math: how to transform a number, say 8, from merely a written symbol to an experience. To enable the students to grasp 8 experientially, teachers encourage them to do 8 jumping jacks, or tag 8 classmates; they divide a pizza into 8 slices. In this way the 8 no longer remains written on the page and in one area of the brain, but becomes experienced; it is something the students get, something they've lived. Here's an example of how we applied this approach when an actress was struggling to believe in her character's experiences as her own.

> YVONNE
>
> When I was twelve, Mr. Yamashida found me hunting through his garbage for something to eat. He could have sent me back to the orphanage. Instead he took me in to his home. (*Sincere, reverential*) In a hundred lifetimes I could never repay him.

When she acted this out, several things were revealed that stuck to the words in ways that popped. Logic tells us that the orphanage must have been pretty brutal if Yvonne preferred to scavenge through garbage rather than go back there. So the actress tried desperately to remain hidden while she scavenged. We had an actor, as Mr. Yamashida, catch her. She cowered and begged him not to send her back. He soothed her and told her not to worry. At that point we had another actor run up as an official from the orphanage and start to roughly drag Yvonne away, at which point Mr. Yamashida intervened. When the official protested, saying that she was a runaway orphan, Mr. Yamashida wrapped his arms protectively around her and corrected him: "She is not an orphan, she is my daughter." As the official retreated, Mr. Yamashida took his newfound daughter into his house. The actress was moved by and believed in those events, because she'd experienced them as actions and essentially lived through them. She knew and was deeply connected not only to what she was talking about but was "sincere, reverential" as well. Acting out the past enabled her to overcome her disbelief.

Just as musicians don't only see notes on the page but hear the music as well, just as those math students no longer see 8 as a figure on the blackboard but as something they've experienced, so too must we actors see not only the words on the page but the life from which they arose—life that has been concentrated into the words but not replaced by them. Just as you would never drink frozen, concentrated orange juice until you had reconstituted it with water, so too must we refrain from tasting the words until we've added *aqua vitae*, the water of life.

How We F.I.O'd the Laid-off Friend Scene

We also applied this active rather than picturing kind of F.I.O. to the dilemma of the actor with the laid-off friend discussed in the previous chapter. Since the actor's choice—using the time he broke his rib, which had nothing to do with the situation he was meant to be experiencing—wasn't working, I asked some of the other actors to play the friend and his children. I had him watch as his friend was fired, how he trudged home, dreading having to break the news to his children. When their dad arrived, his "children" greeted him excitedly, peppering him with questions about when Santa would come and what he would bring; then their father had to break the news and their hearts. All this the actor witnessed and participated in, and because of his ability to make believe, he became so connected to his friend's situation that by the time he had to play the scene, he wept openly, full of compassion and love for his friend. The memory of the broken rib, while "real," had taken him out of the scene and his character, resulting in a concern for his rib, not his friend, which was, after all, what the scene called for.

Fleshing Out the Past via Pictures and Actions

Finally, there's the option of combining picturing and activating when you F.I.O. Not too long ago, an actress came to me for help. She'd booked the female lead in a film, and while thrilled, she was concerned because her entire part was based on the disappearance and murder of her little boy. She and her husband were so devastated that they had made a suicide pact. Obviously her connection to her child had to be incredibly strong. The catch? She'd never had children. So we created a child for her from scratch. She carried him in her belly, felt him kicking, gave birth to him, gave him a name, sang him to sleep, kissed the boo-boo he got playing soccer, loved the Valentine's Day cards he made for her in school, melted when he would put his arms around her neck and tell her he loved her. By this time, because she's an actress, she'd begun to truly believe in herself as a mother and in him as her son.

Then came the hard part. We fleshed out the moment when

he disappeared. They were at a playground, and she had looked down for just a second to check her phone; when she looked up, he was gone. She searched everywhere, thinking he was hiding or playing, just out of sight. When it began to dawn on her that he was missing, she begged everyone around her to tell her if they had seen him, to no avail. We explored her calling the police, having to break the news to her husband, the crushing guilt she felt, and then the dreaded knock on the door, the detectives telling her "We've found your son," and her having to go to the morgue to identify him. When they pulled out the drawer he was lying in, she saw the scar from that boo-boo she'd kissed, and she knew it was her boy.

Around this time she became so agitated she had to stop for a moment to collect herself. She was now not only deeply connected to the child she'd never had but to his murder and the suicide pact as well, without having to access painful, real memories from her real past that had nothing to do with her character's present. Despite the difficulty of what we had created, her instrument was relaxed because the story wasn't real, and yet she connected as if it were.

While sometimes real-life choices are right, the option of F.I.O. means there's absolutely no need to dredge up memories that are best left in the past. Doing so again and again produces tension and an understandable reluctance in the instrument to "go there."

> Is it not monstrous that this player here,
> But in a fiction, in a dream of passion,
> Could force his soul so to his own conceit
> That from her working all the visage wann'd,
> Tears in his eyes, distraction in his aspect,
> A broken voice, an' his whole function suiting
> With forms to his conceit?
>   —William Shakespeare, *Hamlet*
>   (Act 2, Scene 2)

CHAPTER 17

YOUR TEARS ARE NOT ENOUGH

While being emotionally available is definitely important in our craft, there's a lot of confusion surrounding it. For example, there's a perception, shared by many, that crying equates with good acting and hysterical crying with great acting. Nothing could be further from the truth. Hysteria is a state in which your feelings overwhelm your ability to function within the context of the scene. It deprives you, your partner, and the audience of your character's actions, reactions, and interactions. Your performance becomes all about your heaving, sobbing condition and not about your character's situation.

CONDITION (PLAYING YOUR FEELING) VS. SITUATION (PLAYING YOUR INTENTION)

One of my teachers, the wonderful Harold Clurman, often spoke of the difference between condition and situation. He imagined two different scenarios, each involving a man lying on his deathbed. In the first, the man is surrounded by his grieving family and friends, who are crying. He's dying, they're crying, and so on and so on. This, proclaimed Harold, was not theatrical, because everyone involved was merely playing his or her condition (dying, crying). In the second scenario, the man is still dying, those around him are still crying—but he keeps trying to get up and go to work. Now that's a situation that works theatrically and immediately. The man is playing his intention (to go to work), while the others are playing theirs (to prevent him). Each side in the conflict is posing an obstacle to the goal of the other which only strengthens their respective wills. Can you feel how static the first scenario is, with no one wanting to do anything except "feel," in comparison to this one?

Playing a condition (or state of being) as opposed to pursuing an intention has been responsible for the death of many improvisations and scenes. How often have we seen an actor just being drunk, or sick, or tired, or stoned, without doing anything? It grinds the actor to a halt and is boring to watch. And, let's face it, we're often given that kind of direction. But we shouldn't abdicate our creative responsibility and passively acquiesce. Why not, in addition to the "magic if," ("it's as if I were drunk"), apply the "magic although"?: "Although I'm drunk, I still have to perform brain surgery." This is why in class we frequently create "exciting situations" that involve pursuing an intention (doing), after which we just play conditions (being without doing) to feel the difference.

THE GOLDILOCKS OPTION FOR EMOTION

Far too often, actors allow crying to take the place of pursuing intention. But there's also the danger of overreacting in the opposite direction. Being turned off by examples of emotional self-indulgence, many actors decide to avoid the emotional altogether, and like the Devil in Milton's *Paradise Lost*, cite scripture for their purpose in the form of examples of actors who covered their feelings. A former student of mine cited *Terms of Endearment*: "Shirley MacLaine doesn't weep, but you still know she's a tortured, emotional, conflicted and sad soul." But the way to that kind of work goes through the emotional connection, not around it. You cannot cover your feelings unless there are feelings to cover.

I propose a third possibility: neither indulgence in hysteria nor restraint with nothing underneath, but rather making the choices that get you connected to the material without abandoning the pursuit of your intention. If all you're striving for is to feel something, there will be no outward flow of your energy, which will back up inside, clogging you with tension. The word *emotion* derives from the Latin for "moving away from": Your emotions, words, and actions must all be expressive, propelled outward from you, threaded through with what Stanislavski imagined as the "needle" of your intention. If you're deprived of a task, all you'll do is blubber. We've all seen those performances in which the actor didn't want to die, heaving and sobbing through scene after scene. After a while, all of us in the audience had but one thought: *So die already*!

The extent to which you allow your feelings to show is an interpretive choice. If, for example, you want to melt someone's heart, you won't hold back your tears. But if you'd rather die than give the bastard the satisfaction of seeing how much he upset you, then you'll struggle not to show it. Remember, if you're not connected, we won't be, but if all you want to do is cry, we're not going to really care very much about you.

Chapter 18

It's Not a Song Without the Music

Several years ago a student of mine, J., auditioned for the female lead of a film to which many A-list people were attached, including the leading man, screenwriter, and director. While I was coaching her for the audition, we discovered that although the breakdown emphasized her being "sexy" and "edgy," her character was actually involved in a lot of *doing*: defying her carjacker's attempt to intimidate her, rebuffing his advances, etc. Her leading man told her later that while viewing the audition tapes at home, he noticed that his cleaning lady paid no attention to all the other actresses on the tape, who were busy being sexy and edgy, but when J. came on the housekeeper slowed down, started to smile, and finally stopped cleaning altogether and sat down to watch. She went back to work when the tape went back to more women being sexy and edgy. Her costar told her that's what booked her the part. She booked it because she "popped." She popped because she was *doing*.

In the industry, "popping" describes the moment when an actor "pops" off the screen, grabbing the attention of whoever is watching and often grabbing the job (if it's an audition tape) or critical acclaim (if it's an actual performance) as well. This is totally valid: Whom would you hire or applaud, if not the one who popped or, as it's often described, "blew you away"? But there are ways and ways of popping.

Too often I've encountered actors who've been led to believe that the way to pop is through the display of their most attractive physical characteristics. I know there's more of an emphasis on looks than ever before, but why join 'em when you can beat 'em? Assuming you're talented, instead of removing clothing to reveal flesh, why not remove the obstacles to revealing your talent? For instance, resist the tendency to let talking take the place of doing. The word *acting* comes from a Latin verb meaning "to do," or "act," but the ease and clarity with which spoken language can communicate has tempted many actors to allow the rest of their instrument to rest while the words do the work.

Can you imagine going to a concert and having the band only recite the lyrics of the songs while playing none of the music? Wouldn't you feel ripped off? You'd demand your money back, and rightly so, because without the music it isn't a concert, it's only a lot of talk. Far-fetched as this example may be, it's analogous to what I'm encountering more and more, directly and anecdotally, in my work with actors. Rewrite this paragraph's first sentence to read: "Can you imagine watching a play/film/TV show and having the actors only recite their lines while displaying none of their characters' life?" The parallel is exact (except for the "demand your money back" part, since audiences seem more and more willing to accept lifeless recitation as a substitute for acting, as long as the actors are hot).

A short while ago a student of mine was given a monologue to prepare at an audition. After he did it once, the director said, "Now do it again, but this time, create a situation. I don't care what it is, just create one. You can do whatever you want." My student, I'm happy to say, did exactly that. Afterwards the director said, "Wow. I don't know if I should tell you this, but I'm gonna tell you anyway," and went on to say that he had given almost a hundred other actors that same monologue and direction, and every single one of them had said the words in basically the same way as before, with only a change of accent or inflection, instead of creating a situation and living in it.

This is an example of how crippled we've become by our slavery to the words, and how the industry really sits up and takes notice when we bring something to the table that's not just more or different talk. It's shocking how we're treating our work as recitation when it's meant to be action. Our actor's birthright, encoded in our DNA, is the ability to create life, not just say words. We've lost touch with what we did when we were kids—we didn't just talk, we played.

FINDING THE ACTION IN THE SCENE

When we worked on some soap sides in class a while ago, one of the lines exemplified this problem and the solution. A guy sits down, uninvited, at a table where a young woman is waiting for her date to return and comes on to her. She says, "Look, the man whose seat you're in will be back in just a minute." When the actors first encountered this line, they were content to let its meaning do the work for them, and they didn't pop. So we stopped treating it as something to say, and instead tried to treat it as something to do, by uncovering the subtext.

When the actors realized what was really being said ("If my boyfriend catches you hitting on me he'll kick your butt"), they also discovered what was really being done, which was warning. Once they committed to that action, they stopped just talking and started doing and, therefore, popping. Because they were engaged, they were engaging. This, I believe, is an example of Antonin Artaud's goal "to break through language in order to touch life" (see his book *The Theater and Its Double*).

Even improvisation, which Strasberg called the only way to uncover the life of the scene, has fallen victim to this tyranny of talking over doing. Again and again, I have seen improvs reduced to exercises in clever remarks in which nothing is lived or experienced. My student E. went on an audition at which the actors were divided into groups of four and given the situation that they were on a doomed plane. Immediately the other three in her group began screaming—not doing anything, just yelling and screaming. E. took out her cell phone and called her mother. Who do you think got the callback?

Another student, T., wrote to me: "I went on a Global commercial and it was all based on improv. When they told us to improvise, the other girls started talking (not sure why) but I started doing—doing actions. They loved what I did, and I booked it."

Talking Heads

The tendency to let talk take the place of action, of doing, is apparent in many of the actors who audition for me and is something we struggle with in my classes. It has become deeply ingrained, producing a kind of "from the neck up" acting that can't engage us totally, because the actor is divided between the mouth and the rest of the instrument. Stanislavski coined the phrase "the muscles of the tongue" in recognition of the pressure that the words, whether on the page or in the memory, exert on the actor to "Say me, say me!" He likened it to the pressure one feels to put the needle down on a spinning record. (If that image leaves you scratching your head, check with an older person.) We can trace this problem back through the Russian actor-director Meyerhold ("the words are woven on the fabric of the action") all the way to Shakespeare ("suit the action to the word and the word to the action," *Hamlet*). Clearly this tendency has been with us for a long while, and yet, from my perspective, it's growing worse, as actors become increasingly passive in relation to their material. We have to wake up and realize that while we're often intently focused on how we look and clear about what we're saying, we're clueless about what we're doing.

Acting Is Doing

What to do? Let's take inspiration from the professional athletes who hold thousands riveted without uttering a word through the sheer excitement of their actions, which "speak louder than words." What if we adopted a different way of looking at text—sight-reading—like musicians who don't just see the black and white notes on the page but hear the music? Why not have actors see the black and white words on the page and picture behavior, actions, life? Somehow we must cut the loop of "in through the eyes, out through the mouth" that served us well while reading aloud in grade school but which now prevents us from making the invisible visible.

Popping depends on doing, and only when we know what we want will we know what to do to get it. (This is why Russian actors say, "If you don't know what you want, get off the stage.")

Then we have to go ahead and use the words to actually do it. But it requires an instrument whose energy is poised at the point of surface tension, like water risen above the lip of a glass, about to overflow into action despite the limitations of the chair, the room, the frame, or the mark. In fact, those very restrictions can strengthen your will.

As Stanislavski put it, actions aren't always physical; they can be "internal" and "traverse the body but not the space." But you have to see your words as actions to do, not merely things to say. You can hit on someone instead of just saying flirtatious things. You can warn someone instead of just telling them "That seat's taken." (For more examples of internal actions see Chapter 23.)

If all you're doing is talking, your work is going to have a two-dimensional, talking-head quality that just doesn't pop, no matter how hot you are, because talk is indeed cheap and actions do speak louder than words. Just as you can't get blood from a stone, you can't squeeze life from a line.

Isn't it "Lights, Camera, *Action*"?

St. James said it best: "Beloved, be doers of the word."

CHAPTER 19

HOW ORDERING TAKEOUT CAN HELP YOUR CAREER

Fleshing it out, as we have seen, enables us to own references to past events, but there remains the question of how to own references to present ones. When we describe a lover to a friend, we picture him or her vividly as we try to get our friend to see the person we're talking about. Even when we order takeout, we picture what we're ordering. But, as we talked about in the preceding chapter, when it comes to a script we often see only words. To counteract that, I'm proposing a radical transformation of the way actors perceive words on the page.

WORDS ARE CONTAINERS FOR IMAGERY

For far too long, actors have rushed this process, influenced by the frequent direction in the room to "just say the lines," which triggers the fear of taking too long. This has led actors to see the words as literature and to treat saying them as quickly as possible as the be-all and end-all of the acting process, reducing it to a product and themselves to talking books. This approach sucks the life out of the actor's work and the audience's experience, depriving both of the rich imagery inherent in the words. And while this phenomenon is not new (Stanislavski often accused his actors of only picturing the words on the page as opposed to the images they contained), it has been exacerbated by the increasing speed with which technology flashes words across screens, leaving precious little time for spelling or grammar, much less imagery.

Speaking without picturing is neither normal nor natural. Pick up a menu at your favorite restaurant. Even while you're deciding what to order, you're already picturing the choices. Say your mother's first name. Same thing—there's an image attached. We even picture what hasn't happened yet; when we buy a gift for someone, we picture how she'll react before we've given it to her. If a loved one is very late, we picture what might have happened to him. It was Othello's picturing of Desdemona's nonexistent infidelity that led to her murder.

This tendency to picture things is natural to our species. Our visual process begins with the perception of various aspects of a thing (an essentially mechanical step); those aspects are then reassembled in the brain, where emotional significance and meaning are added (an essentially human and, for actors, creative process). This process is reflected in how we learn to read: At first we perceive individual letters, which we sound out to make words, but after a while the letters melt into words, which dissolve into phrases, sentences, and meaning.

I've noticed more and more that the actor's perception of the words on the page still begins with, but now also ends with, that mechanical first stage, after which the actor attempts to add emotional significance and meaning by acting the words rather than reacting to the images that give rise to them. I'm proposing that just as we learn to see the letters melt into words, we allow the words to melt into images. Here's an example from some sitcom sides I coached people on a while ago.

RENEE
(gesturing at her new apartment).
This is my miracle.

KAREN
A miracle is Moses parting the waters. This is just a mess. This is a rough neighborhood, so I won't be visiting you after 6. Wait, is my Benz still out there?

Most actors rushed to say those words, feigning attitudes—"yuck" for the mess, "fear" for the rough neighborhood and "alarm" for the Benz—and turning what should have been a series of experiences into a series of line readings. They had so much more fun when I asked them to choose things to experience in real time that would give them the life in those lines. And they came up with great stuff, once they were allowed to stop talking and picture what they were talking about. Those choices become part of the score, releasing the actors from acting and propelling them toward reacting, from talking to experiencing. Here's how one actress chose to turn those lines into life.

KAREN

A miracle is Moses parting the waters.
> *[Noticing the roaches swarming the leftover pizza in the corner]*

This is just a mess.
> *[Hearing gunshots from outside]*

This is a rough neighborhood, so I won't be visiting you after 6.
> *[Startled by a car alarm]*

Wait, is my Benz still out there?

Try it yourself, first with those choices, then without. I'm sure you'll be able to feel how much thinner it is when you're just talking. And, no, it won't "take too long," because we're asking you to react "as if," not stop the rhythm of the scene while you do a sensory exercise.

THE MAGIC IF

I cannot overestimate the importance of mastering the "as if" reaction, particularly with comedy. It's true that comedy springs from the truth—George Bernard Shaw said that the truth is bitter, so we must make the audience go *"Ha ha ha,"* and when their mouths are open, slip it in. But it's equally true that unless managed carefully, the truth can "kill the funny." The "as if" provides a middle ground. If I say, "This place is just a mess," without experiencing something of the mess, I'll feel fake, because that's a little lie—which, Stanislavski says, will lead to a big lie. It will also expose me to distraction, because nothing will be going on except talking, and I'll have nothing to cocoon me in privacy except the words. If, on the other hand, I grind the rhythm of the scene to a halt while I deeply experience some aspect of the mess—inhaling the smell of garbage, experiencing the greasy grime on the walls, and so on—then I'll have killed the rhythm of the funny and abandoned the genre for drama. The "magic if," on the other hand, "lets the actor off the hook," as Stanislavski said, by lifting the obligation to really, really experience. Instead it permits us to react as if we're experiencing. Try it; it's a tiny difference that makes all the difference in the world. I lose nothing of the rhythm, but now I'm not reciting for no reason. I'm reacting *as if* I smell the garbage, feel the grime, etc.

But remember, you can't be reacting as if you're experiencing if you're only speaking what you're reading or reciting what you've memorized. You must resist the power of the "muscles of the tongue" and instead engage the power of suggestion. If you do, you'll be immediately susceptible to belief in the imaginary, and if you believe, so will we. (As Stanislavski also said, "The small truth leads to the big truth.") If, however, you're only talking, the imagery won't penetrate the words, and your work will never rise above glorified voice acting.

Noticing Between the Lines: Shifts in Mood

This tendency to go to the line readings has brought us to the point where we don't even notice when our lines take a wild jump to something apparently random; we just keep on babbling. Let's look at this example, in which two people are flirting during wartime.

<blockquote>
Lebec
What do you think, Cher? You and me, strolling down Bourbon Street?
</blockquote>

<blockquote>
Dana
You asking me out on a date?
</blockquote>

LEBEC

Sure. First Mardi Gras after the war.

DANA

I've always wanted to see Mardi Gras.

LEBEC

Cher, you don't know the half of it. Party all night long, thousands dancing, makin' love in the soft, New Orleans night air.

DANA

All on our first date, huh?

LEBEC

And it won't be our last.

DANA

You think we'll really live to see it?

LEBEC

Hey . . . you heard what the Lieutenant said. Everybody comes home.

DANA

Would you hold me please . . . just hold me.
(He pulls her to him tenderly.)

Dana goes, in one line, from flirtation to the fear of death, and yet so many actresses, carried along in a rush of words by those muscles of the tongue, didn't even notice that huge shift, and just kept flirting, when clearly the music/atmosphere of the scene had changed.

In real life we're constantly aware of non-sequiturs, instantly reacting with phrases like "Where did that come from?" and "That was random." But, to quote Stanislavski again, "Real life crumbles on the stage." Clearly a choice has to be made by the actress that will shift her that suddenly, but first she'll have to stop talking and notice the shift that's required. In a new twist on "can't get a word in edgewise," we now have actors who can't get a choice in edgewise between the words. This deprives the scene of a change in mood and the actress of the opportunity to reflect the characteristic the casting director is looking for. She needs to choose something to experience that brings her back to the reality of war. And again, once the actors' tongue muscles were stopped, their imaginations started and they made some great choices, such as this example.

LEBEC
And it won't be our last.

DANA
*[her eye caught by the glint of a soldier's bloody
dog tag lying in the dirt].*
You think we'll really live to see it?

Try this yourself, first with that choice, or any other one: She might hear a distant burst of machine-gun fire or the drone of a warplane, or see a bomb explode on the horizon. Any of these and many other choices would do the trick. Now try the sequence again without any choice at all and feel the difference. The lines alone won't do it. As I've said before, you can't get blood from a stone, and you sure as hell can't squeeze life from a line.

Instead, if you listen to and picture what you're saying, images will attach themselves to the words, and the words will attach themselves to your memory, because now they'll be alive in your imagination, not dead on the page, and will, in Wordsworth's words, 'flash upon that inward eye.' And it's not enough to own the images—our job is to give them away, not by speaking to the ears, but to the mind's eye of our partner (and, by extension, our audience). As Stanislavski put it, "your inner vision will awaken ours."

REVIVING "THAT INWARD EYE"

This infusion of words with living images used to be common back when entertainment—reading books, listening to radio dramas, watching black-and-white films—required the active participation of our imaginations. Now, thanks to the amazing effects of digital technology, little is left to the imagination, causing it to atrophy. This is especially evident in the toll it has taken on actors, whose relation to material is becoming increasingly passive. Many actors who, like all of us, picture what they're saying when they're living, are content to merely memorize and recite when they're acting. But we must return to picturing if we truly want to infect both the lines and the audience with life. That's the art, not recitation.

Lines truly are the result of things that happen to us, not of being read off the page or recited from memory. The "mess," the "rough neighborhood," and the fear of losing the Benz or one's life should be experienced in real time, so you're not an actor saying a line but a person having an experience. Whom would you rather watch? Whom would you hire? If we say things our character sees without picturing them as richly as we do an order of shrimp lo mein, it will be painfully clear in the close-up.

SUPPLEMENTAL MATERIAL: LINES ARE THE RESULT OF THINGS THAT HAPPEN TO US

These examples harvested from real life demonstrate what I mean by "lines are the result of things that happen to us." Take a moment to allow the experiencing of the trigger for each of these to flow directly into saying them.

Mmmm, this sweater's so soft.

Is that my phone or yours?

You guys need some cushions on this.

Is John smoking in there?

A little more to the right.

You've really got to take some time to clean this place up.

Did you step in something?

These guys sound good.

It's great to be back in the country.

It's kind of tangy.

Is that who I think it is?

Shhh. I hear something.

Ow, you're hurting me.

It needs a little more garlic, oregano, and fresh pepper.

What the hell are they doing up there? Moving furniture?

The best part's the frosting.

Are you OK?

Whoa. Open some windows.

This is the kind of music that makes you want to be on an island with a piña colada.

It's almost cashmere, but maybe not.

You know, it has a little too much vodka.

Who stepped in shit?

Almost as good as my mother's.

You're glowing.

It kinda has an Indian rhythm to it.

It smells like I'm in the snow.

It's good, but it's kind of bland.

Ugh. This is really sticky.

This table's really smooth.

Wow. It smells like Christmas in here.

I have a bad feeling about this.

Where's that oil smell coming from?

Heather, could you get that?

My ears are so cold, they're burning.

I know you'll feel these are beyond obvious, and it's true that in real life we would automatically experience the triggers for these "lines," but remember Stanislavski's "real life crumbles on the stage." After you've transformed them from lines to life, go back and reduce them to line readings. You'll feel how unsatisfactory yet disturbingly familiar that is.

Part V
In The Waiting Room

All too often the audition is blown in the waiting room. This section shows you how to transform the tension of waiting into something creative.

CHAPTER 20

"THEY CUT ME BEFORE I GOT TO THE GOOD PART!"

The classic actor's lament in this chapter's title is just another way of saying, "I wasn't cooking from the get-go." How is that possible? You're always cooking at an audition—you're nervous and excited, so how can a nervous, excited actor in the waiting room end up boring in the room? By not making those nerves and that excitement work for you *before* you start the scene; otherwise it's too late. All too often the audition is blown in the waiting room. But you can prevent that.

TENSION IS EXCESS ENERGY

First you need to recognize that tension is not some mysterious affliction. It's just excess energy that's getting into trouble, because instead of giving it something creative to do, you're wasting it in a variety of ways, including:

> Playing games or texting on your device.
> Talking with your competition.
> Thinking insecure actor thoughts and otherwise powering the butterflies in your stomach.
> Shaking your wrists, circling your head, etc., in a vain attempt to relax.
> Tightening a straitjacket around yourself, by clenching your jaw, cutting off your breath, or hunching your shoulders up to your ears, so that you're paralyzed.

All of the above have three things in common: They are insufficient to release the excess energy of your tension; they will relieve none of what Stanislavski called "the pressure of having to begin"; and they won't get you cooking. And, as I tell my classes, "If you ain't cookin', you ain't bookin'." (Tacky, I know, but true.)

The Moment Before

We all know that telling ourselves to "just relax," to "chill," doesn't work. We have to offer our energy something more fun, more magnetic, juicier than, say, foot-jiggling or texting. And guess what? That juicy, fun, magnetic option is already there, right in front of you: It's the scene you're about to go in and play. Why wait? Why not start the fun part, the playing (of the part, the scene), right in the waiting room? When you were kids you transformed climbing a bunk bed into climbing a mountain, and crawling under a table was crawling into a cave, so why not transform the waiting room into your character's exciting *moment before*?

No one "enters" from a vacuum except actors. Remember how you could always tell what kind of day your parents had had just by the way they walked in the door? That's because what they had been through came in with them. This is true everywhere you look. Check it out: Watch folks entering an elevator, a party, an office, you name it, and they'll have some kind of state of being because of their moment before. When actors arrive late to coach with me, they always arrive with a very rich state of being: harried, out of breath, sweaty, so they're already cooking by their first "line": "Sorry I'm late." Their state was produced by what they had just been through in their moment before: fuming at the subway while it just sat somewhere, running down the block, trying without success to hail a cab, and so on.

We can always deduce our character's moment before and the state it has produced from our words and/or what others say about us, sometimes even after our character has left. Take this example from a soap: A guy enters and says, "So there you are. I ran over here as fast as I could. I was scared you'd done something drastic to yourself."

Can't you picture his moment before? Something made him fear that the other person, whom he obviously cares about, was going to try to hurt or kill him- or herself. Can you picture the frantic race to avert disaster and the state in which he would arrive? Just thinking about this sequence of events would cause images to arise in the mind's eye of the actor, creating the right state and therefore belief in what he was talking about. Unfortunately, in this case the actor arrived looking perfect, with not one hair out of place, and cool as a cucumber. So from his first line, he wasn't cooking; in fact, he was lying, which was exposed by the disconnection between his words and his lack of an appropriate state.

Have you ever seen a major league ballplayer chilling with his teammates on the bench until he's up, and then running right into the batter's box and taking a swing? No, right? But actors do the equivalent all the time. I'm proposing our version of taking some practice swings, so by the time you're in the batter's box, you've warmed up the very skill set you'll be required to use. It's just common sense, right? And one of the most important areas to warm up is your mind, because where it goes, the rest of you follows.

CHAPTER 21

THINKING THE THOUGHTS OF THE CHARACTER

It's critical for actors to recognize how important it is to combat distraction, one of our primary occupational hazards, by thinking the thoughts of the character. Remember, the very first lesson in Boleslavsky's *Acting: The First Six Lessons* is "Concentration." But we're always so concerned with our lines, our competition, our wanting to book, that we often leave our mind—the thing that can screw us up the most—totally unsupervised, allowing insecure-actor thoughts ("she has more credits than I do," "the whole creative team's in there," etc.) to undermine our focus and confidence. That's why I stress the importance of thinking the thoughts of the character, because doing so immediately crowds out uncreative thoughts and plunges us into the mind of the character and our belief in the very circumstances we're going to have to believe in the audition room.

THE METHOD OF MENTAL ACTIONS

Stanislavski, in his later period, formulated the method of physical actions: What you do and how you do it can stimulate your emotions. This changed the question for the actor from "If you were the character in that situation how would you feel?" to a new question: "If you were the character in that situation, what would you do?" I propose a additional method of mental actions that poses a different question: "If you were the character in that situation, what would you think?" Thinking the character's thoughts will not only protect your mind from distraction and give you belief in the circumstances of the scene, it will actually create the character's emotional connection as well, so you're already experiencing what your character is going through by the time you begin speaking. In addition, this process will yield character, based as it is on mental actions, and actions, says Stanislavski, are thirty-five percent of the part.

In Their Own Words

Rather than tell you myself, I'll let some actors I've coached tell you how they creatively transformed the waiting room and their nervous energy by using their minds to think the thoughts of their characters and their minds' eyes to picture their situations.

> *The audition went great! I had worked on the moment before from the train ride there, all the way up to the waiting room. When I was sitting in the chair I thought about what we had worked on earlier in the day. I saw the guy hitting my pregnant friend in the stomach and saw the blood coming down. I saw him at the bar after-wards with a smirk on his face and surrounded by girls. I saw the banner I made with the word "murderer." I had to hold myself back, I wanted to jump out of the chair! This made me SO angry that I couldn't wait to get in the audition room and tell the police my side of the story, so he could rot in jail. I had so much to think about that I wasn't nervous anymore. I was "thinking the thoughts of the character"!!*
> *A-ha!*
> *I got in the room and my mind was so free that I didn't have to "try" to feel. I felt. The casting director had me walk up to him and pretend to throw a mug of beer in his face, and when he called me "bitch," I wanted to kill him. I remember looking at the casting director with fire in my eyes. And when I left the room, I was shaking! I remembered everything we worked on and applied it. It was so cool. I feel really good about it.*
>
> *—Shannon*

Sitting in the waiting room I once again found myself getting absorbed in the character's thoughts. (It always makes me shake my head and smile to see all the other actors texting or socializing as they wait for their number to be called.) I was thinking how much I, as the character, miss my father. . . . I felt myself getting choked up and I had to back off those thoughts. Instead I sat there as Lucy, waiting for my date to arrive, imagining the waiting room was the lobby of the restaurant he was meeting me at. By the time I went in to read, I was so excited about "my date" . . . that the words just came forth and the connection was immediately there. When I got to the part about "My favorite memories are the stories he would tell me about my Mom" I was fighting not to cry . . . on a first date with a guy who I thought could be "the one."

—Andie

This weekend I shot a pilot. . . . the DP and crew were cranky, rushed . . . making it an INTIMIDATING situation. At first I was thrown by this, but when they were about to do my first close-up I remembered. . . . Think the thoughts of the character. . . . Not only did their frantic energy not touch me but they were even pleased that the director was happy with my shots and we could move on. . . . I believe that thinking the thoughts of the character well before rolling not only gave me focus but gave the people working with me confidence.

—Jenny

Just wanted to let you know that I booked that comedy horror spoof where I felt so relaxed. . . . I realized that I was specific in the thoughts of the character so that without even trying I reacted truthfully. I also got a callback for a short film . . . and I realized that I was . . . thinking real thoughts while the casting director was doing distracting shit. Instead she became "he" and the date wasn't going well . . . so I used what "he" was doing, like at one point while I was speaking she grabbed her coffee cup and the thought quickly flashed into my mind "is he having that bad of a time . . . should I be drinking my drink faster?"

—Nellie

I went to the audition remembering all the things you say about thinking the thoughts of the character. Usually when I go to an audition, and I'm waiting to go, I'm on my cell phone texting or playing tetris. But this time I was like "YO, SON, turn off your fuckin' phone and do this shit correct." So that's what I did. I turned off my phone and started to think the thoughts. . . . I was thinking about my mom getting violated by this man, and my sisters watching and crying . . . and damn if it didn't get me there. . . . So anyway, this is going on in the waiting room . . . and I feel like I'm there! I was so anxious to go into the room and just let loose, and so when I went in, that's what I did . . . thought the same thoughts, evoked the same emotions, and when I was finished there was silence in the room and I still felt the emotions from the visions that I used to make me get to this place. . . . Now I was auditioning for a supporting role in the film. But I got a call today and not only did I get a part in the film . . . I got the LEAD ROLE!!!

—Dartel

I took everything we worked on. . . . Right before I went in I was already thinking about the "ex girlfriend" of my bf that I couldn't stand. Thought about her cheesy clothes and how she thinks her shit don't stink and how I'm going to bring her back down to reality. Then when I went in I took a moment, leaned back on the wall, stared the reader up and down (thinking the thoughts of the character, "who does she think she is?," "look how cheesy she looks," etc.) before I even said the first line. Just got a call from my agent and they are screen testing me for the part.

—Rachael

I had already been thinking the thoughts of the character, so once I arrived outside the building I pretended that I was outside of my new school way too early and had to play the awkward waiting game. I went into the coffee shop next door. Every time somebody walked in I imagined they were a student or faculty member at my new school. I listened to the music my character listens to in the script and I really *didn't feel like "Natalie going into an audition." Even when I went into the waiting room I kept thinking the thoughts of Peyton in a new building. Every time I felt a surge of nerves, I would just remind myself that it was because it was the first day of school. It really, really helped. When I finally got into the room, I felt like I was talking to someone who was on my side rather than across the table judging me. It was as if she was one of my teachers. It felt like a "safe" environment, which usually seems pretty unattainable in an audition room. Moral of the story, I had a really great audition because I used my energy rather than storing it. I felt grounded.*

—Natalie

I got a callback for an ABC pilot. . . . The scene involves me being "walked in on" by my stepmother as I'm having sex, so they were really looking for a genuine reaction followed by an awkward, angry conversation. . . . I spent a long time imagining the shock and embarrassment of being walked-in on, and felt angry and shook up upon entering the room. Needless to say, I kicked ass! Thank you for helping me rid myself of the burden of having to begin.

—Sophia

My audition today at ABC was soooooo much fun! I decided to keep working that idea of living in the world of my story, instead of stressing about the audition. On my way out the door I started thinking about how I need to get to the hospital where my half-sister works to ask her for blood for my father. The train was slow in coming and all I could think was "I need to get there, he'll die today if she says no." When I got to the waiting room at ABC the other actors were hospital patients that had appointments to see her before I went in. The guy who led me in to the audition room was her assistant, and when I finally got in that room, the NEED to say these words to my half-sister, to save my father, was so great, that they poured out of me. I didn't "think about my connection" and "getting into it" as I usually do in the room. The choices we had worked on (the cloudy eyes of my father, holding on to my half-sister's leg and pleading, fioing how horrible he'd been to her and the little things I remembered about how great he'd been with me) they came to me like little snapshots and connected me to what I was saying. When I left the room I was so happy; for maybe the first time in my life I felt great about an audition. And I had no regrets, like so often I do after walking out of the room, feeling that I should have done better. And I had fun!

—*Linda*

I had an audition for an ABC show to be a girl who's being interrogated about the murder of her sister. Waiting in the waiting room all the other girls were glued to their phones, smiling at text messages. I thought the thoughts of my character, acting as if the police were making me wait so they could accuse me of killing my sister. I was pretty pissed off and sad. I thought about my sister's long eyelashes against her cold, dead skin and when I walked into the room I was thinking actively how much I hated the police/friendly reader who was keeping me from grieving. I felt connected. . . . I just got a call saying my manager has an offer for me. I booked it!

—*Kaija*

I auditioned for a play. In the monologue I'm talking to my church's congregation about my brother's grisly death at the hands of insurgents overseas. I often question my ability to deliver emotionally. Not anymore. Instead of mumbling through the words like the other actors auditioning, I filled in the blanks and watched the awful movie in my mind. I walked into that room cocked and fully loaded. The words came out and the tears followed. When I finished the CD looked shaken. He said "thank you" like I had really given him something of beauty. Whether or not I get the part is beside the point. The work transcended the need to be employed in that moment. It was pretty cool.

—*Marty*

I did a scene where I was in an AA sort of meeting but for people that were molested by priests. I pretended the

*people in the waiting room were other kids that were mo-
lested and the reader was my imaginary brother. I was in
full belief of the imaginary circumstances of the scene.*

—*Tommie*

*I got the sides cold and it would have been very easy to
look at the lines and try to work on how best to say them.
But instead I tried to use what we've been doing in class. So
I imagined my moment before, FIO'd the events mentioned,
imagined some other past key events, surrounded the words
with appropriate moving (in both senses of the word) images. I found myself walking into the room with a confident
sense of my personal take on the character that I'd created,
and with surprisingly few nerves, not worried about being
"right, good," rather just keen to share all that was bub-
bling around inside me. And then I was able to just play and
focus on my scene partner and found impulses came to me
that felt right and new and exciting and creative. And it was
a pleasure. Coming out, I felt again that joy and wonder of
the acting experience . . . not at all post-morteming what I
did wrong. People talk a lot about having fun at auditions,
but this time I really did. And it was deeply satisfying in
itself. And then, just as a bonus, the director got in touch
to say she wanted me to play the part.*

—*Paul*

*I wrapped this morning. I got to work with and watch
Michael O'Keefe, Margot Kidder and Michael Buscemi
work. I was treated in a preferential manner and it all felt
like it was because I could deliver. I FIO'd, I wrote out
things I might be thinking about. . . . I was prepared and
thus I got to play when I got to set. When I felt myself slip-
ping into my self-conscious head space I would hear your
voice saying "Think the thoughts of the character" and that
would ground me back in the scene.*

—*Marty*

*I FIO'd everything—the announcement that Miles was
found dead, Colin chasing him, etc. I went to my audition
as if I was walking to the precinct. The linoleum floors, the*

heavy metal doors, it all worked. I was shaking on my way there hoping Colin or his sketchy friend wouldn't see me leave campus. My stomach was in a knot—I had to get this off of my chest if I wanted to make things right. Walked into the room with director/producer/casting assistants sitting there—they were all cops. This was my moment to confess. To make everything right. . . . I flew through it. Out of body experience. I recalled all the memories so vividly that I started bawling at the realization that my call to ask Colin to stop was the reason for Miles' murder. I feel so great. They told me "nice work." I like hearing that. I feel like I really got to the heart of this situation. It all fell together so easily once I'd FIO'd everything. I felt relief like I just left the precinct and made everything right, but also that I went to an audition and believed every word I said. I can sleep well tonight! I feel amazing!

—Sophia

IT'S YOUR TURN

I dare you to follow their example. Stop wasting your precious, creative audition energy in the waiting room on your devices, your uncreative thoughts, and your competition, and instead channel it into thinking the thoughts of your character, creating a moment before. If you do, then instead of being burdened by the "pressure of having to begin," you'll be catapulted into the room with the state of being of your character in the scene, not a nervous actor in an audition. And you will never again be cut before you get to "the good part" because you'll already be cooking, and "the good part" will be from the get-go.

PART VI
IN THE ROOM

How to navigate the many challenges of
auditioning.

CHAPTER 22

CASTING DIRECTORS

At their best, casting directors are gifted matchmakers, blessed with the ability to marry actor and character. Strasberg was right, casting is fifty percent of the show, and that makes CDs co-creators in the deepest of ways. The author has written the characters, the actors bring them to life, and it is the CD who selects those who will give their lives to that cause. For this alone they deserve our gratitude and the title "Director," for so they are.

It is out of this spirit of appreciation that I have put together this compilation, distilled from actors' most common audition concerns, in the hope of fostering greater mutual awareness and understanding between actors and casting directors. To you actors, I offer a few suggestions to enable you to cope with what are often challenging conditions "in the room." Since you're understandably afraid to offend those upon whom you depend for employment, and since I'm ethically bound not to mention names, I must perforce paint with a broad brush here. My focus on negative situations may seem unfair to some casting directors, and, if so, I apologize in advance.

IMPATIENCE AND NEGATIVITY

We all recognize that CDs want to cast the best people for the role, yet we actors often encounter conditions in the room that could (but shouldn't) interfere with our ability to be our best. Sometimes we encounter an atmosphere of impatience. CDs are often under time constraints, but so are film and especially TV directors, and if you're going to act you had better accept that it comes with the territory. No matter how "rushed" you feel, it's no excuse to throw out everything you've prepared. What a great acting challenge for you: to figure out how to adjust to an increase in tempo. There is a wonderful example of how to do that in Robert Lewis's account in *Advice to the Players* of Maria Ouspenskaya's adjustment when told to pick up the pace. She decided that a taxi was waiting for her, its meter running, which allowed her to retain all her choices, while quickening the way she played them.

Sometimes being rushed in the room is accompanied by a negative vibe. No one, in any circumstances, is at their best when feeling intimidated. As Strasberg said, "If you're tense, you can't act." I will never understand the creation of circumstances that obscure the very thing casting is trying to identify, talent. When I have raised this with certain casting directors, I've been told that the roughness of the room can serve as Darwinian selection: only the strongest survive and, by extension, are worthy of being cast. But they're not seeking toughness; they're seeking who's right for the part. And I know from experience that talent will hide when it feels threatened, leaving only a faint hint of the actor's full potential. That can easily happen in an audition, *unless* you are able to immediately flip that negative energy into something creative. Instead of allowing it to jolt you out of the scene, channel it back in. If, for example, it's a love scene, allow the negativity to hurt your character, or smile, knowing it's just your lover's defense mechanism against the vulnerability that love is inducing. But do *not* let whatever you encounter in the room pull you out. Whatever it is, even negativity, is bound to produce strong, truthful stuff in you that can always be poured back into the work in some form or other.

Feedback Too Late

Another concern that's been voiced to me over many years is that while many casting directors give adjustments in the room, to great effect, there are others who seem to think of the audition as a finished product rather than a process—and an opportunity to discover the actor's range. These CDs sit silently throughout the entire audition, and only after the actor has left the room do they say, "he needed more edge" or "she wasn't innocent enough."

Actors bear some responsibility for this, as it is partly the result of the long-term trend of actors painting self-portraits, which has led the industry to believe that what they see is what they get and only what they can get. This orientation unnecessarily extends the casting process and deprives both casting director and actor of the opportunity to work creatively together, however briefly, on the adjustment. I cannot for the life of me understand why, if something is missing, it's not asked for right then and there. So often I've asked, "Did you ask for that in the room?" and been told, "No." But that doesn't absolve you actors of the responsibility to be proactive in the room by asking CDs whether they have any adjustments for you. Exhibit a willingness to engage, to take direction, to demonstrate other sides of yourself. What's the worst they can say? "No."

While this lack of engagement in the acting process can inhibit creativity and delay casting until the callback, it's even more serious when there is no callback, because the actor has been rejected for not delivering what he or she was never asked for in the first place. This can be enormously frustrating. A student of mine, whose sense of innocence is readily accessible, went in for a part that was described as "tough and edgy," which is how he played it. He received no feedback until his manager called to tell him he didn't get the part. Why not? "You weren't innocent enough." That's not only the actor's loss, but the casting director's and the project's as well, because by never asking for what they wanted, they never got to see what he could give. But there's no telling what might have happened if he had asked them if he could try it again, differently.

FOCUS ON YOUR WORK, NOT THEIR WORDS

Finally, in the crucible of auditions, you are bound to imbue any reaction directly concerning your work with overwhelming significance. Even the most casual interaction can be parsed endlessly for meaning. ("She didn't say anything right away after we finished. I really think she was involved in what I did." "He didn't look up when I said 'good-bye'—he hated me.") I regularly have to talk actors down by trying to translate remarks that unintentionally caused agita due to a lack of a common lexicon of acting terms. Just ask the actress who to this day is puzzling over feedback that pronounced her "like red earth." Even a seemingly unambiguous reaction can turn out to be misleading: An actor who made those in the room laugh so hard they cried and hugged him afterwards, showering him with effusive praise, afterwards heard from his agent that they found him "too green."

In light of this, I urge all of you to make certain that your work, not the CDs words and reactions, is the focus of your attention. If you've truly done your best, then you can let it go. If there are things you did that left you feeling dissatisfied, consider the audition a useful learning experience and make avoiding those missteps your goal for next time. I speak from experience. In the very early days of Lincoln Center I blew an audition, badly, and not for the first time, because I shrank in the room. Sitting outside by the fountain I vowed that I would never again have the explosion outside afterwards ("Damn it! What's wrong with me?!?"). From then on, for better or worse, I exploded in the room and was able to walk out free of "woulda, coulda, shoulda."

Also bear in mind that often a word and/or behavior can carry widely different connotations for speaker and listener, casting director and actor, even two actors. I'm reminded of the anthropologists who landed their helicopter in a previously unexplored region and were met by the indigenous population running at them, shaking their fists. The explorers took off in a hurry, only to discover later that the behavior was a sign of the most cordial welcome. Or take the famous Broadway composer and lyricist Frank Loesser, who, I've been told, was always curt to those he was going to cast and lovely to those he wasn't. When asked why, he explained that those to be cast were going to get their reward, and he wanted the others to get a little something as well.

So let your work speak for itself, confident that if given half a chance, you can surprise them ("I didn't know the kid could do that"), because you have the universe inside you.

CHAPTER 23

"ACTING IN QUOTATION MARKS"

"Acting in quotation marks" is a phrase Bertolt Brecht used for the way people describe something intense that they have experienced or witnessed. Let's say a passerby sees a car crash. In conveying what she has witnessed, she will neither say the words dispassionately nor enter into the full experiencing of the event the way the victims (or an actor) would. Agitated by what she has just seen, the passerby will find neutral speech insufficient to convey the intensity of the scene. Her description will be charged with the excitement she's feeling, resulting in a kind of acting out, not a full version, but one in which gestures and behavior are employed to augment the normal mode of speech. She may use one hand, for example, to indicate the direction one car was going in, the other to show the path of the second car, then *Wham!*—both hands exploding together to convey the impact when the vehicles crashed into one another. This middle ground between full experiencing and mere talk is "acting in quotation marks."

TRAVERSE THE BODY BUT NOT THE SPACE

This seems to me as good a way as any to describe the strange style of acting required in an audition ("in the room"). It's "strange," because you want to be at your fullest, but at the same time you do not want to get such feedback as, "The kid was all over the place" or "He was hiding behind the props" or "She was too big for the room/frame." Conversely, you do not want to be so afraid of being "too big" that you end up being frozen and not living in the situation at all. There is a third possibility, and that's where the "quotation marks" style comes in.

I don't mean that we would act in the room like a witness on the street describing a car crash. I use that example only to suggest a kind of acting in which the experiencing is full, but its expression is concentrated; a style of acting wherein large human experiencing is compressed into actions that, as Stanislavski put it, "traverse the body but not the space." And this approach can also be applied on set, where the limitations of the frame often require it.

Years ago I coached a young actress on her first feature. Her character had been raped and in a later scene was forced to encounter her rapist. While her natural reaction would have been to flee when she saw him, the shot required her to stay in frame and not move. Since she was seated on a sofa when she saw him, I asked her to take the energy of her fleeing impulse and channel it into pressing herself against the sofa—that gave her the full experience of shrinking from him without actually fleeing out of frame.

For another film, an actress had to watch her lover drive away, perhaps forever, while she had to stand at the curb and say good-bye. To her it felt wrong, under the circumstances, to just stand there, so I asked her to explore what she would do if she were really in that situation. Immediately she began to run after the car, calling out her good-byes as she ran. When it was time to shoot, that action was still going on inside of her, despite her having to stay on her mark and in the frame.

EMBRACE THE LIMITATIONS OF THE ROOM

Both of the situations I just described exemplify that principle of having the action "traverse the body but not the space." You can apply this in the room as well, but first your instrument has to be in the right state, both mentally and physically. Mentally, we often inhibit our ability by thinking, "Fine. If I can't do it fully, then I won't do it at all." This approach results, of course, in exactly that, and doing nothing at all rarely gets a callback, much less the job. It's important to embrace the limitations of the chair, the mark, or the frame as an obstacle that, as Stanislavski said, "strengthens the will."

Physically, it's important that your instrument be on the edge of its seat—not sunk back as if in an overstuffed armchair—on the brink of doing, not talking. Begin by immediately exploring the full version of the action, so that you can arrive at the condensed version. It's pointless to try to restrain something if there's nothing to be restrained. Once you've explored the reality of the fully executed action, then (and only then) it will be possible for you to condense it. Can't you picture, in both examples, how those actresses, while sitting on the couch or standing on the sidewalk, weren't just sitting or standing? One was shrinking from a rapist, the other struggling not to run after her lover—actions that were literally going on inside them and expressed through their energy, their vibes, and their eyes, despite not coming out in space. Stanislavski called this phenomenon "static rhythm"; it's how you sit or stand differently when you're expecting your lover to come through the door than when you're expecting a tiger.

This is easily transferred to the room, where strong limitations apply. You will pop if you're doing (see Chapter 18) and you won't if you're not. Once you're really doing, in real time, despite restrictions, you'll believe in yourself, your situations, and your actions. And if you believe, we will; if you don't, we won't. And belief, Stanislavski reminds us, is essential for inspiration.

CHAPTER 24

WORKING WITH A PARTNER

Partnership takes many forms. In Chapter 3 the role of the partner was played by the gazelle. In the two chapters that follow this one, you'll encounter many more references to partners. With monologues, the imaginary person you're addressing is your partner, (unless you're specifically asked to engage with the CD, agent, etc.) With sides the reader is your partner, and in a scene the other actor is your partner. Whatever the material or situation, the partner gives you the impetus to transform the material from something to say to something to experience, liberating you from acting to reacting. And it can transport you from just understanding the situation to connecting to it. When we get to Chapter 26, we'll practice with some sides in which the situation is "love at first sight." OK, we all know what that means—but only when you choose a real or imaginary partner to experience it with will your juices begin to flow.

PICTURE THE PARTNER

I often give the instruction "picture the partner" (as you will see in the next two chapters), but with a couple of admonitions. Don't take this literally, as one young woman did, who interpreted that to mean she should stare at a still picture of the person she chose. And don't try to force yourself to hallucinate that the reader or your scene partner really is whomever you've chosen. That will only undermine your belief, which will create tension in your instrument. Instead of hanging on white-knuckled to your choice of whom your partner is, treat the reader or your scene partner *as if* they're who you need them to be (real or imaginary), with the light make-believe of a child.

I have often used my mother as an illustration of this approach when confronted with a young actor who's having difficulty believing in his (or her) partner. "Let's say I have to play a scene with my mother and you're my partner," I tell the actor. We agree he looks nothing like an eighty-one-year-old woman, but, I assure him, "through the power of the 'magic if,'" I'm going to believe enough in you as my mom that I can play the scene." I then proceed to behave the way I would when she was alive: I immediately try to improve my hair, my clothing, and my posture—all things she insisted on, even at the end. Then I adopt the calm, soothing tone I always used with her, and inquire, "Mom, how are the legs?" By that time, I'd have sufficient belief to play the scene without once trying to trick my eye into believing that the twenty-something actor was an octogenarian.

PASS THE PARTNER THROUGH YOUR IMAGINATION

Let's say you're in a scene in which you're confronting your wife with her infidelity. If you've been cheated on in your past, treat the reader or your scene partner as if she's that woman. If you haven't had that experience, then choose someone you care about and react as if she or he had betrayed you. This will prevent you from relying on the real person's limitations and protect you from the eternal complaints that "the reader gave me nothing" and the other actor is "wrong for the part." When you ingest a mint it dissolves into your bloodstream, and a similar thing happens when you pass a real person through your imagination: You end up with neither her wholly real self, nor wholly whom you've chosen her to be, but a third, as yet unknown possibility, a hybrid. (See also Chapter 10, where we discuss making the same adjustment to your character.)

Just today I received an urgent email from a student on set, whose acting partner, while meant to be her best friend from childhood, was resisting the bonding that could lead to such a relationship. My advice to her was to pass the other actress through her imagination, fleshing out (F.I.O.'ing; see Chapter 16) the hurtful events in her past that had made her so standoffish, which aroused my student's compassion and understanding. Thus the real person, by virtue of the imagination, dissolved into the bloodstream (and heart) of my student, becoming who she needed her to be.

THE PARTNER IS YOUR KEY

Keep in mind that this process of choosing your partner is designed not to lock you into a choice but to unlock the situation for you, to disclose its meaning in ways that you can connect to, so you can say to yourself, "Oh, *that's* what's going on; this is like when my brother. . . ."

Finally, the choice of a partner can also unlock your character for you. It can save you from either losing yourself by pasting on some sort of external, clichéd Romeo, or losing Romeo by bringing him down to your self-portrait. Instead, ask yourself, "Was there ever a Juliet in my life?"

Your partner is your freedom. Your partner is your peace.

CHAPTER 25

MONOLOGUES

Countless actors have told me they hate having to deliver monologues. This hatred, however, comes from a misperception of monologues as chunks of words recited in a vacuum in which the actor feels utterly naked, deprived of anything to hold onto. If this were indeed the case, I wouldn't blame them for their hatred. But it's not.

CREATE THE SITUATION

No one wants to see you recite memorized words. That is neither interesting nor fun for you or whoever is forced to watch you. This is why a casting director once told me, "I'd rather crawl on my knees over broken glass than listen to a monologue." To make it more interesting for you and your audience, why not perceive the monologue as a situation rather than a recitation? As soon as you're experiencing the juicy situation that's the source of your lines, you'll be reacting your way into the words from within—you'll be interesting because you'll be interested. There's no way around this: If we want to be riveting, we must be riveted. The alternative is just tedious.

I recently worked with a young man, L., who began his mono-logue, and he was sad. Boy, was he ever sad. As the monologue went on, he continued to be sad as he recounted various horrors he'd experienced. But nothing was going on, because he wasn't involved in a situation, so he didn't want anything, and since he didn't want anything, he wasn't doing anything except saying his words sadly, playing his condition. This is anti-theatrical (in a word, *boring*); never play your state/condition (see Chapter 17). If you do, you'll end up like L., sad at the beginning, sad in the middle, sad at the end, with no arc, no situation, and therefore no reason for talking (intention). Remember, as I've said elsewhere, lines are the result of things that happen to us.

In an attempt to rescue L., I asked him about the situation his character was in, and we discovered that he was trying to get his girlfriend to understand why he was unable to be loving and affectionate toward her. Did L. have a girlfriend that he cared about as much as the character cared about his? Yes. (If he hadn't, we'd have made her up.) Then we had an actress play his girlfriend. She tried all sorts of ways to get him to respond to her hugs and caresses, and when it became clear that it was hopeless, she gave up and began to walk out. Suddenly the material came alive in L., and he used the words to get her to see and understand what he'd been through that made it so difficult for him to love. He was no longer just being sad, he was trying to stop her from breaking up with him. The match of his talent was ignited by the striking surface of the situation. It was thrilling to watch.

Therefore, before you start focusing on the lines and (God forbid) how you think you should say them, ask yourself, "What's going on?" If you can answer that in a juicy way that grabs you, you'll play that, not your condition, or your words—which, by the way, will come out just fine once you're connected to the situation. L. never once had to worry about a line reading: He was too caught up in trying not to lose his girlfriend. And doesn't it feel much more fun and exciting to think, "I'm going in there to try to stop my girl from leaving me," than "I'm going in there to recite my monologue"?

FIND YOUR INTENTION

This choice also enabled L.'s monologue, although mostly about the past, to still occur in the present, so something was actually going on in real time. No matter how much the lines spring from the past, keep in mind you're still saying them in the present. You should ask yourself, "Why am I talking?" and your

142

answer must never be "Because I memorized these words, and some stranger just told me to start reciting them." If you have no reason for talking, we'll have no reason to listen.

I love the concept of what linguists call a "speech act." It replaces the false division between passive speaking and active doing with a dynamic hybrid in which words become actions for accomplishing things in real time. In this case, L. was suddenly engaged in pursuing an intention—trying to stop his lover from leaving him by means of a series of speech acts:

> Pleading with her to stay.
> Trying to get her to understand what he'd been through by
> Picturing the horrible images from his past that had snuffed out his ability to love and then trying to
> Get her to see them in her mind's eye and
> Using them to soften her heart.

This choice also gave L. the thoughts he'd think before saying his first line. He'd no longer have to stand there thinking nervous actor thoughts, and he had too much at stake to waste his energy that way. Instead he could condense his thoughts along these lines: "Oh, God, she's leaving me," which would plunge him, body, mind, and soul, into the high-stakes situation, and he'd be catapulted into the monologue.

MONOLOGUE AS DIALOGUE

Because we had improvised the moment before his girlfriend's leaving, he knew which reactions of hers to choose to feed his belief in, and connection to, the situation. Again, he wasn't hallucinating, merely reacting to the power of suggestion, as if she were putting on her coat, taking off the ring he had given her, and walking to the door. This leads us to another misconception actors have about monologues: They're not monologues at all; they're dialogues.

I often have to remind actors of this. Sometimes the dialogue arises from the partner's behavior, as is the case in L.'s monologue. But the dialogue is also sometimes evident in certain lines that are clearly in response to something the partner has said or done. Most actors typically rush through those lines, depriving themselves of the logic, belief, and support that experiencing the trigger would provide. A line like, "No, Jim, don't interrupt me," for example, obviously arises from Jim's starting to say or do something to interrupt. Experiencing that little truth, small as it is, can (recall Stanislavski's words) lead to a bigger truth: that the actor is involved in a situation (dialogue), not just a recitation (monologue). (In addition, those lines will be impossible to forget, because they'll be attached to something experiential, not just the page or your memory.)

Conversely, to say such a line without experiencing the attempted interruption becomes a small lie that leads to a big one. On top of which, it's really crazy to say such a line for no reason. If we did in real life, our Jim would wonder, "Where the hell did that come from?" But actors do this all the time (real life crumbling again.) I'm not suggesting that you attempt to hallucinate that Jim was about to interrupt but, again, that you react as if he were. Do this lightly, with a child's sense of make-believe. Part of your talent lies in your sensitivity to the power of suggestion, so you don't need to force anything.

WHERE TO LOOK

A question actors often ask, and about which there is much disagreement, is: Where should you direct your eye line? Often actors have auditioned for me without a clue, and when I've declined to be their partner have announced, "I'll just look at that spot on the wall," which is as boring as it sounds. While I understand the desire to look at the person who's auditioning you (he or she is, after all, real), that choice can be problematic. There are folks who request that the monologue be delivered to them, but the vast majority, in my experience, prefer not to be corralled into partnering you. Some find it uncomfortable, while others, myself included, find that it makes evaluating actors' work more difficult when you're forced to meet their eyes instead of perceiving the bigger picture.

Remember as well that though a real person, the auditioner

has not rehearsed with you. By making her your partner, you've made yourself vulnerable to her behavior (yawning, looking at her watch, writing on your resume). It is far better in my opinion to have chosen your partner in advance, someone who's just right for the piece, and to picture him or her on one side or the other of the auditioner, or the camera if one is involved.

SUMMARY

Here's a quick checklist of the steps we've covered in this and preceding chapters to help you prepare to deliver a monologue:

Perceive the monologue as a situation to experience—not words to say.

Cocoon yourself from distracting thoughts like "What are they writing on my resume?" by thinking the thoughts of the character, even in the waiting room.

Create a moment-before that catapults you into the situation, not just the words.

Choose a loaded partner—real, imaginary, or a "combo platter" (where you pass a real partner through your imagination to make him or her more suitable)—and turn the monologue into a dialogue as if the partner's reactions with words and/or behavior at strategic moments   impel you to talk..

Choose a juicy intention and execute the speech acts to achieve it.

If you follow these steps with any monologue, instead of reciting words in a vacuum, you'll be living through a sequence of experiences, as in a movie. Trust me, that's more fun for everyone.

One last thing: So many actors drop the last line of their monologue like a hot potato and whip around to see my reaction. This undermines their work in several ways: Ideally you've cast a spell during your monologue (the original meaning of "a spell cast" was "a tale told"), and you shatter it by coming out of it so quickly. Additionally, this is an industry that is wary of neediness. I have often heard from casting directors "the kid was too eager to please" or "the kid was too desperate." By immediately looking to your auditioner ("Did you like it? Huh? Huh?"), you're coming across as exactly that. Remember, in this business (as in matters of the heart), if you crowd your partner, he or she will retreat from you.

CHAPTER 26

SIDES

Let's try something. Before you read through this chapter, look over the sides below and then tape yourself doing them, trying to ignore everything else on these pages, including the numbers I've added to the text. Later on you'll retape to compare.

Now, having done that, chances are that to a greater or lesser extent, you relied on one aspect of your talent that can be dangerous: your unconscious tendency to say the lines with the clichéd, "natural" line readings that come so easily to us but that strand you in talk. In being so quick to say the lines, we drown out what they're trying to say to us. By immediately starting to act the words we start to harden them into line readings that might not have anything to do with the actual logic and reality of the scene, and a vocal pattern, once established, is very hard to break.

Instead of starting with how the lines should come out, why not unlock the text to focus on what causes them to come out—namely, the situation. You know that expression "You can't see the forest for the trees"? For actors that means don't pay so much attention to the trees of the lines that you lose sight of the forest of the situation. With only the lines, you'll be a deer in the headlights, public in public, prey to all sorts of distractions. Cocooned by the situation, you'll be a deer in the forest, private in public. It's similar to what I notice, or rather what I don't, when walking our dogs: While I only see the surface of the bushes (the "lines"), Cookie, Willie, and Chase are alive to all the events that have left traces on those bushes; they can smell them and it excites them. The bushes' importance is derived from the life they're marked with. It's the same with lines. If we only see the lines and fail to catch the scent of the exciting life they contain, that's like mistaking the tracks of the animal for the animal itself. So read the sides not just for the meaning of words, but for a whiff of the clues they've been brushed with that will reveal the situation.

EDIE

So what's your story, Tim?

TIM

Story?

EDIE

I don't know, what do you do? [1]

TIM

I'm a video-transcriber. Sort of a glorified typist. What do you do? [2]

EDIE

(almost to herself)
I don't know why I asked you that.

TIM

We have to say something, right? [4]

EDIE

(Laughs a bit, then)
Right. [5]

TIM looks at EDIE. EDIE looks at TIM. There is an attraction. [8]

EDIE

Listen, I gotta go. [7]

TIM

If you want, I could walk you— [16]

EDIE
I have to meet someone.

TIM
I'll walk you there then, if— [17]

EDIE
It's my boyfriend. [3]

TIM
Oh. Okay, well.

Tim looks around and takes a deep, long breath.

TIM
I just uh . . . [13] I enjoy talking to you.

EDIE smiles, flattered, but she knows what's happening here. [14]

EDIE
Thanks, but um—Sometimes when I get reckless, I get in trouble. [15] Sorry, I just can't. [18]

EDIE shakes her head, looking down, then looks at TIM. Her eyes glisten in the streetlight; she's holding herself back. TIM seems to understand and looks away with regret; [6] then

EDIE
Maybe in another life. [19]

Tim looks up and smiles a little.

TIM
(warming to the idea)
Yeah. Okay. That'd be great. [20]

EDIE
Right. Okay then . . . [21] Well, goodnight.

TIM
Tim. [22]

EDIE.
Tim. [23] Okay. Bye.

TIM
Take care. [24] See you in another life. [25]

> *EDIE walks away, turns the corner, goes down
> some steps leading to an apartment building. She
> searches through her bag and pulls out a set of
> keys.*
> *Int. Steve's apartment living room. Night.*
>
> *EDIE lets herself into an expensive loft [10] and
> takes off her shoes. High ceilings, skylights. Most
> of the walls are covered with paintings. Across the
> room STEVE sits at a desk talking on the phone. He
> kisses EDIE quickly while still talking on the phone.*

STEVE
(English accent)
. . . I'm not the one being difficult. [12]

> *STEVE, forties, has a shaggy crew cut. His paunch
> and wire frame glasses make him look older, but
> he is hip, with a few rings on his fingers and a
> confident swagger. [9]*

STEVE
(grabbing EDIE's hand [11])
Hey. You want to order takeout?

THE SITUATION

What are the clues that can reveal the situation? Well, first of all, Edie and Tim have only just met. How do I know this? Because she doesn't know what he does (1), and he doesn't know what she does (2) or that she has a boyfriend (3), two of the first things we find out when we meet someone attractive. But it's not as simple as boy meets girl. Check out the stage directions (6) after she says "Sorry, I just can't." She "shakes her head, looking down. . . . Her eyes glisten in the streetlight" (meaning there are tears in her eyes), "she's holding herself back. Tim . . . looks away with regret." Those are pretty strong reactions from two people who have only just met. How do we explain this? What do we call this when there's such an intense connection between two strangers? Love at first sight? *Bam.* That's the situation. And knowing that, we now know many things, such as how to behave. (It's the same as when I know I'm going to a funeral, or a club—I don't need an acting coach to tell me how to dress or behave.)

Knowing that it's love at first sight also tells you who your partner is. If you're Tim, ask yourself, "Have I ever fallen in love at first sight? Was there ever an Edie in my life?" If you're Edie, ask the same questions regarding Tim. If the answer is yes, that's who your Tim or Edie is, and all you need do is treat the reader as if he or she were that real person. Some actors have answered, "Not love but very strong attraction at first sight," which has always seemed to work perfectly well for them. For those who have never experienced anything remotely close, make it up. Often actors have lit up when asked if they had a fantasy or dream lover, which has also worked very well.

There are two more things the situation can yield: atmosphere and the moment before. Deer-in-the-headlights actors wait in a vacuum for someone to tell them to start talking. If you're a deer-in-the-forest-of-the-situation actor, however, you're no longer in the room, you're in a juicy situation: falling in love at first sight. Even in the waiting room, you're not wasting your talent or energy texting or playing games on your devices—instead, you're creating the imaginary circumstances you're going to have to experience in the room. In this situation, make believe you've already caught a glimpse of the other and are dying to get in the room to talk with him or her. Meanwhile, you can be thinking your character's thoughts: "Damn (s)he's cute. I can't believe how I'm feeling. I've got to say something."

Once in the room, take a moment to experience your Tim or Edie and to think the thoughts and behave the way you did when you first laid eyes on him or her (or the way you would if you had) right into your first lines. This will envelop you in a rich and private atmosphere, which Stanislavski said should "pour like smoke off the stage" and will, in addition, produce behavior, which the director Elia Kazan called "psychology made visible." This way you're already riveting (because you're riveted) and are popping even before a line is spoken. In addition, you're satisfying the first sides of the character as reflected in the sides, romantic, flirty, sexy.

UNLOCKING THE TEXT

Can you tell, however, that everything—characteristics, atmosphere, music—changes after Edie says, "Right" (5)? At first, she "laughs a bit," because Tim's "We have to say something, right?" (4) is an acknowledgment of the intense energy between them. Can you sense that they'd explode if they both just stood there silently? Then, in the midst of her laughter, as they look at each other, experiencing their mutual attraction, something happens. As we said in the previous chapter, notice when a line is clearly the result of something your character is experiencing; do not blindly say, "Listen, I gotta go" (7) for no reason at all except that it's the next line. Ask yourself, "What makes me have to leave *there*, not earlier or later, especially right after 'There is an attraction' (8)"? Again, lines are the result of things that happen to us, and it's part of your skill set to stop the muscles of the tongue and notice when something changes. This will require some serious unlocking of the text.

Jump to the section after Edie and Tim's dialogue stops. (Always read everything before and after the lines of the scene.) See how her boyfriend Steve is described as in his "forties" with a "paunch" (potbelly) that makes him "looks older" (9)? Didn't you get the impression that Edie is young and attractive? But notice, Steve has an "expensive loft" (10). OK, this is an old story, but there are darker tones as well: He grabs her hand (11), has a "confident swagger" (9), is having an icky conversation on the phone (12), and doesn't seem to value her for who she is. When Tim tells her "I enjoy talking to you" (13), which is pretty generic, she "smiles, flattered" (14), so we know that she's starved for even that little bit of validation. My sense is that Steve values her more for sexual, rather than verbal, intercourse.

But darker still is her line, "Sometimes when I get reckless, I get in trouble" (15). Tim hasn't proposed anything more reckless than walking with her, but as far as Steve's concerned, walking with another man is "reckless" behavior and can get her in trouble. This makes sense for Steve: He knows she's a hottie, that she's with him partly for the comfortable lifestyle he provides, not his youthful physique and good looks, and that men will hit on her when she's out by herself. Logic tells us, then, that Steve is jealous and controlling. An actress playing Edie will have to flesh out (F.I.O.; see Chapter 16) the situation underneath that line, by drawing on her imagination and/or on any experiences of jealous men in real life to picture what happens when she walks in the door even a few minutes late (maybe he's waiting, ready to pounce with the interrogation, "Why are you late? You met someone, didn't you?"). This will cause images to arise that enable her to know what she's talking about, and we'll see it in her eyes.

Now we've unlocked enough to make some choices as to what Edie experiences, in real time, that makes her cut short the love-at-first-sight "attraction" with "Listen, I gotta go" (7). She could, for example, see Steve's best friend across the street ("Uh-oh, what if he tells on me?"), or her phone could vibrate. She wouldn't even have to look at it to know it's Steve, checking up on her. He keeps her on a short leash. Either choice (or others) would totally and organically change her focus from Tim to an urgent need to go (to avoid getting "in trouble"). Meanwhile, the music of the scene has darkened, along with the second set of characteristics the sides are looking for: Tim is worried he'll never see Edie again, which is why he twice offers to walk her

(16, 17); she's worried about being late, and Tim's picking up on that and is concerned for her. It's that concern that makes him stop himself from saying something more intense than "I just uh . . ." (13), like "I just fell in love with you." Of course he wants to tell her how he feels, he's fallen in love with her and now she's leaving, but in those three dots he sees she's too distracted/agitated to hear that. So, out of love for her, he puts her needs before his own and resigns from telling her how he feels, saying "I enjoy talking to you" instead.

In order for Edie to truly "smile" and feel "flattered" (14), she should flesh out a few situations in which Steve clearly had no interest in what she had to say, making her feel as if she had no value except as a sexual object. In this way, Tim's words will feel like water for her thirsty soul. With her "reckless . . . trouble" line (15), Edie is trying to get Tim to understand, and with her "Sorry, I just can't "(18) she's apologizing for having to ruin something so special between them. Then, she must first experience how Tim "looks away with regret" (4), in order to turn her next line, "Maybe in another life" (19), into the action of giving him some hope, no matter how far-fetched. She needs him to know, before they part, that she feels the same way, and that if it were up to her, they'd be together. Tim must also turn his line, "Yeah. Okay. That'd be great" (20), into an action of realizing that the feeling is mutual and grasping at the slim hope she's holding out, in order to "smile a little" and warm to the idea. In the ellipsis (21) before Edie's "Well, goodnight," she should be trying to memorize his face, for all too soon that will be all she has to remember him by. Tim should use his line "Tim" (22) as an action, to burn his name into her memory, so she'll never forget it. She does so in replying, "Tim" (23). We can tell how hard it is for her to leave by how broken up the rest of her line is: "Okay. Bye." Tim's "Take care" (24) is not the throwaway it could've been without the unlocking we've done. Now, having seen her anxiety/fear, he can use that line as an action, to urge her to protect herself. "See you in another life" (25) becomes an action as well, to hold her to her earlier promise, "Maybe in another life" (19).

PLAYING THE PART

Now it's as if we've just had a coaching session, and it's time to retape yourself, which presents another danger: trying to "do it right" by trying to act every single note given above. This is truly the best way to kill your acting impulse and any joy you might have in the room. The coaching is like weight training to strengthen your forearm so your tennis serve is faster. It makes sense. What wouldn't make sense would be if you brought the weight out onto the tennis court and held onto it as you played. And this is ultimately about *playing*, a part, a scene. Having been coached, go in there and play; some of the choices we've made will stick, and some won't. No worries—nobody bats .1000, or even .500 for that matter. But when you compare the before and after tapes of this scene, I think you'll agree that your second version has more often than not turned the lines into life, and while there are a million folks who can say lines, those who can create life in the petri dish of the room or on set are very special indeed.

CHAPTER 27

OFF YOU GO . . .

You cannot develop your talent and neglect your humanity. With talent comes responsibility: to reveal the truth, not display yourselves. Acting is not about you, it's about what Helen Hayes called "adding something to the lives of that audience out there." And audiences need you more than ever as they drown in the welter of their devices. To whom can they turn to remind them of their humanity, if not you? But you can't feed their souls if your own is starving—overfed and undernourished by the fast food of "communication" technology.

Let's try something. Disconnect from your devices for a moment and become still, really still. *Shhhhhh*. You can text them all later. Now, listen to your blood memory as if it were a seashell pressed to your ear, and you will feel stirring within you the ancient acting potencies of your magical actor-race. You are called. Reclaim your job, which from forever has been to make the people more humane by the humanity of your work. Reprise your role as runways of the human spirit. You are the sons and daughters of shamans and sorcerers, actors lit from within, whose signals through the flames can light the world.

And remember: despite all the stuff that can (but shouldn't) get in the way, your work is to play (a part)—so it's meant to be fun.

Make your contribution. You are called.

Break a leg.

BIBLIOGRAPHY

Some of the quotations that appear in this book come from encounters with those quoted, while others were passed to me anecdotally. The chapter "Anne Frank Wasn't Hot" appeared in slightly different form in *The Washington Post* on June 8, 2008, under the title "Face It. It's Not About Talent." Jennifer Aniston's anecdote in chapter 9 is printed here with her permission. The "In Their Own Words" emails in chapter 21 have been used with the permission of the actors who sent them to me. The various sides and snippets from audition materials that I have used throughout the book have been passed on to me over the years by students, casting directors, and others; I regret that I am unable to credit their originators.

I've compiled here a list of the sources I used in writing the book, as well as a selection of further readings. I apologize in advance if I have missed acknowledging or crediting any contributions.

Artaud, Antonin, and Mary Caroline Richards (trans.). *The Theater and Its Double*. New York: Grove Press, 1958.

Benedetti, Jean. *Stanislavski and the Actor*. New York: Routledge, Theatre Arts Books, 1998.

Boleslavsky, Richard. *Acting: The First Six Lessons*. New York: Routledge, Theatre Arts Books, 1933.

Borny, Geoffrey. *Interpreting Chekhov*. Canberra, Australia: ANU E Press, 2006.

Brecht, Bertolt, and Eric Bentley (trans.). *The Caucasian Chalk Circle*. New York: Grove/Atlantic, 1971.

Campbell, Joseph. *The Masks of God*. Vol. 1, *Primitive Mythology*. New York: Viking Penguin, Inc., 1959.

Chekhov, Anton. *Plays*. New York: Penguin Classics, 2002.

de Mille, Agnes. *Martha: The Life and Work of Martha Graham*. New York: Random House, 1991.

Eliot, T. S. "The Hollow Men," *Poems: 1909–1925*. London: Faber & Faber Limited, 1933.

Eliot, T. S. *The Rock: A Pageant Play*. London: Faber & Faber Limited, 1934.

Esslin, Martin. *Brecht: The Man and His Work*. New York: Norton, 1974.

Kazan, Elia. *Kazan on Directing*. New York: Alfred A. Knopf, 2009.

Kuhn, Herbert. *Auf den Spuren des Eiszeitmenschen*. Wiesbaden, Germany: F. A. Brockhaus, 1953.

Lewis, Robert, and Harold Clurman. *Advice to the Players*. New York: Theatre Communications Group, Inc., 1980.

Masefield, John. "Sea Fever," *Salt-Water Ballads*. London (Chiswick): Chiswick Press, 1913.

Miller, Arthur. *The Crucible*. New York: Viking Press, 1953.

Milton, John. *Paradise Lost*. New York: Penguin Classics, 2000.

Molière, and Richard Wilbur (trans.). *Tartuffe*. New York: Harcourt Brace & Company, 1963.

Osborne, John. *Look Back in Anger*. New York: Criterion, 1957.

Pound, Ezra. *Instigations of Ezra Pound*. New York: Boni and Liveright, 1920.

Rothenberg, Jerome (ed.). *Technicians of the Sacred: A Range of Poetries from Africa, America, Asia, Europe and Oceania*. New York: Doubleday, 1968.

Shakespeare, William, and W. J. Craig (ed.). *The Oxford Shakespeare: The Complete Works of William Shakespeare*. London: Oxford University Press, 1914.

Stanislavski, Konstantin, and Jean Benedetti (trans.). *An Actor's Work on a Role*. New York: Routledge, 2010.

Stanislavski, Constantin, and Elizabeth Reynolds Hapgood (trans.). *An Actor Prepares*. New York: Routledge, Theatre Arts Books, 1989.

Stanislavski, Constantin, and Elizabeth Reynolds Hapgood (trans.). *Building a Character*. New York: Routledge, Theatre Arts Books, 1949.

Stanislavski, Constantin, and Elizabeth Reynolds Hapgood (trans.). *Creating a Role*. New York: Routledge, Theatre Arts Books, 1961.

Stanislavski, Constantin, and J. J. Robbins (trans.). *My Life in Art*. New York: Little, Brown and Company, 1924.

Strasberg, Lee, and Robert H. Hethmon (ed.). *Strasberg at the Actors Studio: Tape Recorded Sessions*. New York: Theatre Communications Group, Inc., 1965.

Thomas, Marlo. *The Right Words at the Right Time*. New York: Atria Books, 2002.

Toporkov, Vasili, and Jean Benedetti (trans.). *Stanislavski in Rehearsal*. New York and London: Routledge, Theatre Arts Books, 2004.

Williams, Tennessee. "Lament for the Moths" and "The Dangerous Painters," *In the Winter of Cities*. New York: New Directions, 1956.

Anthony Abeson's high school summers were always spent in summer stock, acting and directing, along with all the other jobs summer theater required: stage managing, set construction, lighting design, etc. Teaching surfaced even then. His earliest memory is of writing the name "Konstantin S. Stanislavski" on a blackboard in front of bewildered children's theater apprentices.

While at Columbia University he made his off-Broadway debut as an actor and assistant director at the Sheridan Square Playhouse in a repertory company whose director introduced him to Lee Strasberg and the Actors Studio. He was unable to attend his graduation due to his appointment by the Queen Elizabeth II Arts Council as a resident actor and director of the Canterbury Theatre Company in Christchurch, New Zealand, that country's first international, professional theater, where he worked with actors from all over the U.K. (As a twenty-two-year-old American, it was a challenge to direct actors whose previous director had been Laurence Olivier.) While there, Anthony also served as the director of the Experimental Theatre Laboratory of the Christchurch Academy of Dramatic Arts, that country's first training academy.

In 1968 he began his long collaboration with Jerzy Grotowski, first as an actor at the Centre Dramatique National du Sud-Est in Aix-en-Provence, and later, in the early 1970s, as a participant/assistant in Grotowski's first "Special Project" in a forest outside of Philadelphia. Further collaboration occurred under the auspices of the Instytut Aktora in Wroclaw and Brzezinka, Poland.

In 1972 Anthony was invited to join Peter Brook, former director of the Royal Shakespeare Company, at his Centre International de Recherche Théâtrale, in Paris, where he participated as an actor in the Centre's exploration of the effect of nonlinear language on the actor's process. The research was facilitated by the deliberate inclusion of actors from Japan, Africa, France, and other countries, with hardly any common language between them. Instead, during Anthony's stay, the verbal impulse was channeled into ancient Greek and/or bird calls and applied to situations created by Ted Hughes, Sylvia Plath's husband, who went on to become the poet laureate of England.

In 1968, Anthony started a theater company, the Ensemble Theatre Laboratory, a project of both the New York State Arts Council and the New Mexico State Arts Commission. One of its founding members was the late actor-monologist Spalding Gray, whose ironic version of their Missouri tour of *The Tower of Babel*, can be found in his *A Personal History of the American Theatre*.

During this time, Anthony continued to be exposed to Lee Strasberg and the Actors Studio, becoming one of the youngest people ever to address a special session of the Studio with Lee. As a member of the Directors Unit of the Studio, he was taught by Harold Clurman. He was honored to have been a guest in both their homes.

In 1973 Anthony began another theater company, the Washington Theatre Laboratory of Washington, D.C., with the support of the National Endowment for the Arts and the D.C. Arts Commission. The company's training program marked the start of many careers, including those of Caroline Aaron and Karen Allen. Selected as a seminal archetype of the experimental theater movement in America, its archival materials are housed in the permanent collection of the Jerome Lawrence and Robert E. Lee Theatre Research Institute at Ohio State University.

Returning to New York, Anthony studied with Stella Adler at her conservatory and joined the faculty of the Drama Department of the High School of Performing Arts, where he first worked with Esai Morales, Reno Wilson, and Jennifer Aniston, among many talented others. Jennifer, who went on to study with Anthony in his adult classes, wrote of her experiences with him in Marlo Thomas's book *The Right Words at the Right Time*. While at the school, Anthony was selected from the combined faculties of the Performing Arts and Music and Art high schools to be awarded the first Manhattan Superintendent's Award for Excellence in Teaching.

For more than twenty-five years, Anthony has been an acting teacher and coach in New York City. His work has been documented in the Emmy award-winning episode of Bill Moyers's PBS series *Creativity*, the Ace award-winning Manhattan Cable Television documentary *Chasing Dreams*, and the BBC documentary *Bus and Truck*. He has been interviewed on E! Entertainment, Shine Television of England, as well as A&E's Biography network. As an author, Anthony has been published in the *Washington Post*'s Outlook section, the *Village Voice*, the *Washington Star*, and the *Theatre Paper*, as well as in numerous online publications. Many of his acting students have gone on to successful careers in theater, film, and television.